dis.con.tinued

"dissed" *by man*
"continued" *with God*

Fernando E. Franco Sr.

FIRST EDITION
https://www.onlinechurchgrowthmaterial.com/

dis.con.tinued

Published by ocgm.publishing
Printed in the *United States of America*

ISBN PRINT: 978-0-578-53674-3
ISBN EBOOK: 978-0-578-53821-1

Cover design by Richell Balansag

Photography by sillypandamedia.post.pro

Religion, motivational, leadership, spiritual

Follow Pastor Fernie

On Instagram
@pastorfernie

On Facebook
Fernie Franco Sr.

On Youtube
https://www.youtube.com/user/ThePASTORFERNIE

Dedication

To my exquisite, beauteous wife Veronica.
You are the "SUITABLE" helper that God blessed me with.

CONTENTS

ACKNOWLEDGEMENTS

To my family

My wife Veronica, My son Fernie Jr., My daughter Destiny, My daughter Hannah, My son Nehemiah (R.I.P) My grandson Angel, My mother Charlotte, My father Mondy (R.I.P.), My sister Monica, My brother Armando, My mother-in-law Rosie (RIP).

You all have allowed me to share my life with so many others aside from you.

To my team at CityView Worship Church of Oxnard.

You have remained steadfast through the ups and downs on our journey. You are the ones that make the church soar. We finally can say *"our team is now the size of our dream."*

To my church - "CityView Worship Church of Oxnard."

You show up week after week, you serve week after week, you love week after week, you make me smile week after week. Some of you stuck like "crazy"-glue through all the "craziness," and others who walked into a wounded and perplexed church were patient enough for us to heal.

I pray blessing over you always.

When asked to read this book by Pastor Fernie, I thought to myself, *if it isn't good how do I tell him?*

Shame on me. It has never been about Pastor Fernie from preaching in front of thousands all over the world to one-on-ones with everyday people seeking God's comfort. This book is a true reflection of the person behind a purpose and that's to spread the gospel.

Dis.con.tinued offers insight into a seasoned pastor's journey from a leadership favorite to the subject of criticism and eventually being discontinued. It is a reality check for every person who claims to serve God: when things do not go as we expect they would, can we separate God from the actions of men?

In this book, you will find the balance between Pastor Fernie's real life experience and God's word and guidance. It is rare that you find leadership so transparent in times of uncertainty. What makes this a book a must read is its authenticity and sincerity.

Pete Salgado
TV Producer, Manager to Fernando Vargas, and the late Jenni Rivera

Dis.con.tinued (Definition) "*... to put an end to;*
expired or *no longer available or produced.*"

O ur church was so excited when we received news that multiple pallets of decorative stunning wood flooring was donated. What appeared to be so valuable was not so! For an irresistible price, we posted it on social media platforms such as Letgo, Craigslist, and OfferUp. To our amazement, people looked at the decorative wood flooring but did not want to BUY! We then began to offer it for free, and still no response.

We later found that people were uncertain of purchasing because this remarkable decorative wood flooring was **dis. con.tinued.** This meant if the customer would purchase and begin to install the flooring and didn't have enough, it would not be possible to order the remaining balance needed to complete the flooring job. It was **dis.con.tinued.**

It's so interesting to see how people who at one time were considered *valuable* to friends, people, family, can go from *wanted* to dis.con.tinued. Today, we see this happen in the entertainment industry. When their song was #1 on music charts, they were so valuable. When their song was no longer played on the airwaves, they were forgotten. Furthermore, if their song was a "one hit wonder," the world just seemed to forget that they were even in existence. Have you ever heard the saying, "Where are they now?"—I'll tell you where! **dis.con.tinued.**

> *It's so interesting to see how people who at one time were considered valuable to friends, people, family, can go from wanted to dis.con.tinued. —FF*

We see the same happen with actors in the film industry. At one time they were a number one choice for nearly almost all executive producers and motion picture parent companies. Today, they're no longer chosen, let alone nowhere to be found! Why is that? **dis.con.tinued**.

Perhaps you're in a divorce recovery, lost friends, or have recently been terminated from a career. If you just have the feeling that you're **dis.con.tinued** or have been told you're **dis.con.tinued**, I have great news for you!

Keep reading this book and in spite of how EXPIRED you feel or think, you'll witness one chapter at a time on how you

> *You can go from dis. con.tinued to dancing, from dancing to dan.SING! —FF*

can go from dis.con.tinued to dancing, from dancing to dan. SING!

You may have been **"dissed"** by man, but not by God. You are NOT **dis.con.tinued!**

CHAPTER ONE

DIS.CON.TINUED

"Just when I thought I was soaring!"

Many people reading this book may have felt the pain of being **dis.con.tinued**. If you've ever gone through a divorce, you may have felt like you wasted your time with your then-spouse, maybe even having believed at one time that you were no longer good for anybody else. If you've lost a child through death, there's the sense that you can't live on. If you've lost a house by way of foreclosure you say, *Now what am I going to do?*

I don't know what you may be experiencing in your life during this very season. Perhaps you feel like you just don't have enough oxygen to walk one more mile… or even one more step. But you discover yourself reading this book because it has been *appointed by God* that this book find you somehow, somewhere, right now. One thing I do know—*It's not a mistake* that you are about to read a story that will give you wings to fly again, breath to run, and life that will drive you back with pleasure to thrive!

Dis.con.tinued. That was the harshest word I have ever received; it came by way of an agonizing and disturbing letter from the *Church Organization* that I had been serving for

> *You are about to read a story that will give you wings to fly again, breath to run, and life that will drive you back with pleasure to thrive! —FF*

thirty-one consecutive years of my forty-seven years of life, beginning when I was just sixteen-years-old! This was the ONLY fellowship I had ever belonged to. In due course, after demonstrating leadership, loyalty, and faithfulness, I had been promoted to a top-level position, which involved overseeing multiple churches in the prepossessing state of California. I was honored at what came next—becoming a keynote speaker at conferences with over ten thousand in attendance, and many other conventions. Eventually I spoke across the United States of America to South Africa.

While I was away from my house one day, the infamous white, purple, and orange FedEx truck pulled up to my front door, and the driver asked my son to sign for a certified letter. When I arrived home later that day, I opened up that letter and my stomach flipped; the FedEx driver might just as well have kept the letter and run me over. It was the most surprising, disturbing, and downright agonizing letter I had EVER received in all my years of ministry!

The letter read, in part:

> *Taking into consideration the entirety of the situation at hand it has been decided to serve this notification to advise you that "your church" will be <u>discontinued</u> with the organization effective immediately.*

The words pierced my body, spirit, and mind like poison-tipped arrows. **Shock. Confusion. Pain. Disorientation.**

Essentially, I was being *"put to an end; or no longer available to produce."* Thirty-two years of service! How could they do this to me? My wife Veronica, my children, and I tried to faithfully demonstrate loyalty and faithfulness to this organization. I really believe that conceivably thousands of people think we left the organization out of disloyalty, but the truth is, I was asked to be **dis.con.tinued** immediately. And to this day—every time I talk about it, I get sick to my stomach. *Every* time!

As a pastor, father, husband, and a human being, I have faced many battles throughout my life in ministry:

- Three heart attacks.
- Directing a Rehabilitation Home twenty-four hours a day with NO pay, NO gas, NO food, NO government assistance, NO transportation…

because this was part of my training to become a pastor.

- Accusations and surprising backstabs from some of the people closest to me.
- My wife's diagnosis of leukemia.
- The miscarriage of our child Nehemiah Hunter due to my wife's cancer.
- My father's death from lung cancer.
- My mother-in-law's death of a hemorrhage in her brain.
- My eleven-year-old daughter gone missing, becoming a teenage mother.

The list could go on for a few more pages... *but the biggest heartbreak of all was receiving that LETTER in the mail that said my church was being* **dis.con.tinued.**

Throughout my thirty years of full-time ministry with the organization, I must have attended well over one hundred meetings face-to-face. Sat with the president and top leadership to plan, strategize, raise capital funds, and contribute to the growth of this worldwide organization. When I received that letter I just kept asking myself, *WHY? WHY?* The least they could have done was to dial ten numbers so we could arrange to meet in person one last time, or even just talk via phone; it should have been the most important conversation in all our years of bonding.

Why couldn't they just tell me directly to my face? WHY? Why am I being **dis.con.tinued?** The letter never gave me answers to my questions, and to this day I still do not know why!

You may be a young Christian reading this and the experiences I'm describing could be disturbing your new walk with God. You may wonder how one Christian can do this to another? Aren't we supposed to be in unity and love? Yes, we are! But please keep in mind that this book is not written to discourage nor **denigrate** one another or the organization I once belonged to.

This story is not to tell of what *"THEY"* did to me but what *"IT"* did to me. I will talk more about this in the next chapter.

> *This story is not to tell of what "THEY" did to me but what "IT" did to me. —FF*

CHAPTER TWO

HATER-ISIM

Some of what "they" really say is true.

I know we were all born a human being, but sometimes it's hard being human. I'm human, my family is, my church is, and so are you. Even Jesus was human, though "divine" was also attached to his title. *He was tempted in every way that we are, but he did not sin* **(Hebrews 4:15)**. One of our disadvantages as humans is that you and I are NOT divine! And because we are merely human, there will always be someone who is judging you or perhaps you may be the one who is always doing the judging.

> *There will always be someone who is judging you or perhaps you may be the one who is always doing the judging. —FF*

Apparently, there were some financial accusations against me: concerns of unaccounted-for money, missing money, misuse of money. Rumor had it that I had absconded with up to three million dollars.

Three years before those accusations began, we were out of the country, as always with the top-level leadership of the organization. I was sitting under the president's visionary preaching of the growing of megachurches. Finding myself enthused, challenged, and passionate to respond, I returned home to California and met with some of our leaders. I shared what I had heard God say to me very clearly while I was out of the country: "*If you don't sell your building and purchase a bigger one, your church is going to die.*"

At that time, my church was holding three services on Sunday as well as one midweek service and close to one hundred small group gatherings. We were experiencing exponential growth and had no more space for kids, congregants, parking, or even administrative staff. Approximately two years after that word from God, we sold our building and became a mobile church. This was a huge transition for us after having owned our previous church home for approximately twenty years.

As time went on, some of the congregants began to get impatient, and that's when the accusations, plotting, and secretive planning began to unfold. Truthfully, I don't blame some of the individuals behaving in this manner. We hadn't bought another building, I had some nice stuff, I was traveling the world preaching, and I had found favor with the organization. So I can understand where the discontent was stemming from, but most of it was so unnecessary and hurtful.

The number of disgruntled and concerned people began to grow *(they had every right to their opinions, but God is the righteous judge)*, and eventually a group of them flagged the attention of the headquarters, which took appropriate action by issuing an investigational financial audit. After a long seven-week process, the headquarters received *"clean"* audit results—far from the rumor of me taking millions of dollars! *The top paragraph of the CPA's "Final Thoughts" read:*

> *"There are no large obvious fund transfers from the church's account to an individual's account."*

When the audit was completed, my wife and I were called to the headquarters for a meeting. The conclusion entailed an agreement to keep me as lead pastor of my church with certain applicable restrictions.

Two weeks later, two of the organization's leaders visited my church and conducted a members' meeting to inform the congregation of the results of the audit. It was mentioned that I would remain as lead pastor.

But just three days later I received that *letter.* I'm getting *sick* again at just the mention of it.

I didn't know what to do!

In the beginning stages of learning how to lead, when people started to criticize, judge, and comment on my perceived weaknesses and character, I would immediately become defensive and deny that what they were saying was true.

I guess I thought I was a perfect person in my earlier years of life. Judgement is especially hard on those who preach the gospel, lead in the church or workplace professing to be a Christian. I constantly have to remind myself what James 3:1 says: *... for we who teach will be judged more strictly.* Some of the judgement comes from people who love you and some comes from those who dislike you.

> *Some of the judgement comes from people who love you and some comes from those who dislike you. —FF*

It's very difficult at times to refrain from speaking when tempted to judge a person who is in the wrong or even at times with those who may be perfectly innocent.

> *It's very difficult at times to refrain from speaking when tempted to judge a person who is in the wrong or even at times with those who may be perfectly innocent. —FF*

I have to say that probably one of the biggest mistakes that I had made was not effectively communicating with my parishioners during the building project. The people weren't seeing the progress they were hoping to.

We had signed a lease agreement to purchase an industrial building. The challenge we were facing was that we couldn't set foot in it until we qualified for a loan. We then needed construction plans approved that will pass through our city, then begin renovation to obtain an occupancy permit. When the lease agreement came to fruition, I hadn't had a ton of experience with leading up to that point. I'm pleased to say today: we got the loan to purchase the building one day after our discontinuance and we are 90% complete with construction!

As I sit and remember the love I had given to some of those dissatisfied people, I'm going to be honest... after all these years in ministry, I still say to myself, *How can they say those things about me, let alone believe them to be true?* It's a possibility that some may have indeed felt the absence of *my love* towards them, and maybe even my lack of people-skills (from what some said). And some of them may have been absolutely right, but I just couldn't understand how they could unite with those who were willing to be part of a church split! It hurt Veronica and I so bad, and it still does to this day. I'm sure they also hurt bad and perhaps are still hurting also.

Truly, I can say there is no bitterness in my heart towards anyone in my life who have **"dissed"** me, and I pray the same for those who feel they've been "dissed" by me, although I can also say that I still pray for them.

I still remember the day when I answered the call of God to be a pastor. I remember praying to God and asking

Him to confirm if I'm really to be a lead pastor. I can still hear His voice as I was in a deep, reverent time in prayer—and GOD answered *YES, I have called you to be a Lead Pastor.* Then He said to me as clear as He could sound, "I have called you to love the people but I am not promising that they will love you back." Whoa! What a true word from the Lord! I

> "I have called you to love the people but I am not promising that they will love you back."

didn't totally understand all of what this would warrant, but twenty years later I can tell you what God meant. If it were not for those words that the Lord had spoken to me as a young man, I would have given up when my closest friends decided to leave the church.

> It is not an enemy who taunts me—I could bear that. It is not my foes who so arrogantly insult me—I could have hidden from them. Instead, it is you—my equal, my companion and close friend. What good fellowship we once enjoyed as we walked together to the house of God. —Psalm 55:12–14

The 55th Psalm explains exactly my lament: It is not an enemy who taunts me—I could bear that. It is not my foes who so arrogantly insult me—I could have hidden from them. Instead, it is you—my equal, my companion and close friend. What good fellowship we once enjoyed as we walked together to the house of God.

I've learned a long time ago "don't keep score with the people you serve, because the day they leave, you won't have reasons as to why they should stay."

As a pastor, it can be very difficult at times to avoid keeping score with people because of all that you do for them.

I can remember throughout all my years of pastoring...

> *"Don't keep score with the people you serve, because the day they leave, you won't have reasons as to why they should stay." —FF*

- Being called upon by married couples well past midnight to intervene in their marriage.
- Hugging, embracing people as their diseased loved ones took their very last breath.
- Counseling long hours and offering many prayers for people.
- Taking people on trips across the country.
- Countless numbers of hospital visits.
- Overlooking people's shortcomings, loving them through it all, not holding any wrongdoing against them.

I know what you may be thinking right about now. You're thinking that I'm keeping score! I really don't mean to sound like I am, I'm just sharing with you what many pastors do for their people. He loves them unconditionally just like Jesus loved His sheep.

I had no other experience outside this fellowship. I **actually believed the letter!** It made such an impact on my life that I thought I was done, that it was over, the calling of being a pastor was finished. Honestly, I thought I wouldn't have any other favor outside of that organization; I didn't think I would even have a following if I didn't remain in the same organization.

During the lengthy audit investigation, that organization planted a new church just nineteen miles from where I was conducting my services. This is not a long distance away from my small city. They have such a loyal following that I thought all of my church members would transfer to the new church plant. During that time, I listened to Satan's intimidating and familiar voice. *I had no chance at all* if I began a new ministry. However, in the letter they sent me it read I was to be **dis.con.tinued** immediately!

Immediately after I was **dis.con.tinued**, our Friday church service was approaching just two days later. I still didn't know what I was going to do. I wasn't going to try and call all of my congregation on the phone to explain to them one by one about the **discontinuance**. There were too many to call, and I wanted to look at them **face to face** and read the letter to all my congregation at once.

At the Friday service, I told my congregation that they needed to return in two days for our Sunday morning service, make contact with everyone they could, and inform them about a special announcement I was going to make during that service. I wanted as many people to be present as possible. Sunday arrived about as fast as a lightning strike. I was so nervous on my way to church as thousands of scenarios raced through my mind. But I found enough strength to read that letter word for word from behind the podium.

After I read the letter and caught my breath, I shared three invitations: *First,* those who chose to follow our previous organization, we would bless them and harbor no ill will; *second,* those who felt they needed to find another church, we would bless them as well (many chose one of those invitations); the *third* invitation was to those who felt led by the Holy Spirit to start a part of a then no-named, wounded, and disillusioned church to see what God would do. *Honestly, at that point, I wasn't even sure if I was still going to pastor.*

I am grateful to say that many chose to stay with us on this faith journey.

I tried my best to model Christ by setting an example on how to be a leader that would love, forgive, understand, and not harbor any form of bitterness during this period.

Now I know what to do!

From the time of the Friday service to Sunday, my feelings were to retreat and passionately seek the face of my maker so I wouldn't make any foolish decisions! It's amazing how in life you get so used to going to people for all your answers. I'm not sure if that's how you are but this is what I was used to doing for thirty-one years, then I finally realized that I had NO ONE.

All my friends, my pastor, my pastor's friends, and clergy were now out of my life. The reason being was nobody's fault but my own. The only friendships I had developed were within the fellowship. I had just one person I could talk to and that was my best friend, the one that sticks closer than a brother—JESUS CHRIST.

After speaking with my Lord and Savior, I then spoke with my wife and informed her of what the Lord was directing me to do; He was directing me to pray and fast immediately. She felt the same way. Veronica told me to take as long as was needed to retreat and seek. Veronica had gone to speak to her parents the day after we received the letter. She informed her parents of the discontinuance. Her mother was a faithful woman of God who served in her same church for thirty-eight consecutive years. She looked at Veronica in the eye and said boldly, *"Daughter, man didn't call you and Fernando, God called you two!"*

On that Sunday, I told my congregation that I was going to need to separate myself unto God and seek the Lord with all my HEART as on what He would have me to do? Immediately after church, I traveled to a peaceful and coastal city, locked myself in a hotel room so it was just me and God. No interruptions from my family, church, anyone.

I asked God if he could just answer two things I needed to know before the five days of prayer and fasting were over:

Am I still called to pastor?
If I am, what would the new church name be?

After the first three days the Lord spoke to me and said, "I have called you to continue to pastor, even if it's just five people who remain with you; I have called you to pastor those five people."

> "I have called you to continue to pastor, even if it's just five people who remain with you; I have called you to pastor those five people."

Having a peace in my heart, I slept very well that night. In the morning, due to the slightly opened drape curtain that hung across the window, and the sun shining bright on my face, I woke myself up!

Desperately, I dove back into prayer. I needed to hear from God in regard to my second petition. I said, *"God, I have peace in my heart about remaining in the call and position of pastor. Father, I now need to know—what is the name of our new church?"* After many more hours of praying, I am now asking for some names that would be the perfect fit for the culture and the heartbeat of our congregation. I felt led by the Holy Spirit to contact my inner circle of leaders for help. I asked them all to send in some of their best ideas of what the new name of the church would be. Together, we came up with a total of forty-seven names for the church and narrowed it down to just two.

It was a difficult choice to make, however, after confirmation from God, we indeed made the right decision on what is known today as **"CITYVIEW WORSHIP CHURCH OF OXNARD."** It wasn't as easy as I thought it would be!

SUICIDAL THOUGHTS

I was raised on the other side of the railroad tracks till the age of twenty-three. Almost anyone who is raised on the other side usually comes from a dysfunctional family (at least in my neighborhood, I did). Abandoned by my father just before my teenage years. My mother played dual roles (dad and mom); she had no transportation and we survived off of government assistance.

Our house was old and beat down with two car jacks holding up our front porch. We couldn't afford a carpenter. There wasn't even plumbing, so we would have to place plastic garbage bags in the toilet bowl and make sure they were tied on pretty strong. My job was to empty those bags when they were filled with waste. When it came time to bathe, we would heat up four big pots of water on the stove and pour them into the old cracked bathtub to bathe. We had no shower, rats ran around the house in broad daylight, and there was a beehive in our kitchen walls. Masking tape kept the bees from entering the inside of our house, although one day they did escape—must have been over five hundred bees that caused us to evacuate, and we ran down our block on Hayes Ave. as if it were our last day of life! Raised on government cheese, unsweetened corn flakes, white-labeled peanut butter, and worst of all—**low self-esteem**. At least low self-esteem for an American. You know what I'm talking about if you live (or have lived) on the other side of the tracks in the United States.

The honest truth was my living environment was so embarrassing; I was fatherless and ashamed. If my friend's parents dared to cross the railroad tracks and give me a ride home, I would have them drop me off at a nicer-looking house that wasn't mine. When they drove away, I would then walk into reality at 414 N. Hayes Ave.

One day I was at a friend's house who lived in the better part of my city (northside). As I was playing and running around the inside of his house having fun, he then yelled at me from the top of his lungs, *"Hey! Stop running around in my living room. You don't see me running around in your house! First of all, there's no room to run around in your house."* As a child, not knowing then, this affected me so severely; I didn't have a clue as to the extent. I had no idea how it would later on in life carry over into adulthood. I didn't know that this, and a lot of other garbage I carried around since childhood, would end up being a psychological issue in my life until I received that *letter*.

That letter made me feel abandoned. But this time it came from a spiritual father, the thousands of friends, hundreds of clergies I gelled with in the course of me being part of the fellowship—now, all gone. NO where! NO calls! NO emails. I was abandoned once again.

I felt like an orphan and my church was nearly aborted. When a child is an orphan, he don't care what color are the hands that feed him. Even if it's the Devil's hands!

> *I felt like an orphan and my church was nearly aborted. When a child is an orphan, he don't care what color are the hands that feed him. Even if it's the Devil's hands! —FF*

About three months after I was **dis.con.tinued**, the media television networks nationwide were broadcasting a certain season of **"Pastor Suicides."**

Church members often don't realize what some pastors would dare not to admit. Statistics about pastors and depression, burnout, health, low pay, spirituality, relationships, and longevity say that 70% of pastors constantly fight depression, and 71% are burned out. Meanwhile, 72% of pastors say they only study the Bible when they are preparing for

> *Statistics about pastors and depression, burnout, health, low pay, spirituality, relationships, and longevity say that 70% of pastors constantly fight depression, and 71% are burned out.*

sermons, 80% believe pastoral ministry has negatively affected their families, and 70% say they don't have a close friend.

Surprisingly, our greatest example, Jesus Christ, was even faced with the decision of suicide! Matthew writes: *For the second test the Devil took him to the Holy City. He sat him on top of the Temple and said, "Since you are God's Son, jump,"* (MATTHEW 4:5).

> *Surprisingly, our greatest example, Jesus Christ, was even faced with the decision of suicide! —FF*

Again, where the hurt comes from is how we as pastors still love, receive, look beyond other's shortcomings, sacrifice, and would think parishioners would do the same for us—**WRONG!**

I was extremely downcast during the time of the pastor suicides. All that kept going through my mind was that I was **dis.con.tinued** from my "organization."

Little by little the same suicidal spirit was now taking possession of my life. Remember what the **Dis.con.tinued** definition reads? "… *to put an end to; something that is no longer available or produced.*"

I was feeling like a NOBODY without the "organization." I had been wanting to tell Veronica for so long about Satan's spiritual attack of **PASTOR SUICIDE** on my life, I already was depressed, and I didn't want to look like a weak fleeing coward!

During this time, I was left without a pastor of my own, no personal covering over my life. I did, however, have an inner circle team of the pastors in my own church that I held myself accountable to, but this attack on my life was too shameful for me to tell anyone at that time.

One day, Veronica and I were having lunch in Nipomo, California, and my eyes began to water and swell as the meal was being brought to our table. She asked me what was wrong and I said I'd rather talk to her in private away from the restaurant. We left the restaurant and drove to only God knows where in that tiny town. I pulled over and parked on some desolate side road, pure silence on my part, tears couldn't stop running down my face. My wife had NO clue as to what it was that needed to be said. I finally pulled out enough courage to confide in my wife (who was, at that time, the ONLY person I could 100% trust after all I had been through). I was so ashamed, embarrassed, and fearful to tell her. But at the same time, I was also so terrified of the *thoughts* I was having of taking my own life.

This was Satan himself attacking me! No demon, evil spirit, it was SATAN himself trying to kill me. The scripture in the gospel of John became so real to me, as it says, *The thief's purpose is to steal, **kill**, and destroy* (**John 10:10**).

It took me about half an hour in that car before I could even get the first word out of my mouth. Finally, the Holy Spirit gave me the ability to express to her the THOUGHTS that had been plaguing my mind. I didn't want to be another pastor on the news—my wife a widow; my children and grandchildren without a role model; our church kids left without their pastor lost, confused, and questioning God. My very own mother had just lost my dad in death one year prior, and her mother died just three months after my father. Losing her son would have been way too much and undeserving for my beautiful mom. **This was real! It was close!**

I just couldn't get over how abandoned and alone I felt. I was astonished because all those years the fellowship embedded in us that we were *family*. As I told Veronica more details of those attacks, I could tell she was so *shocked*, even though she didn't show it. She didn't know what to say, but her being the lovable strong woman of God—she just sat in that passenger seat, watched me cry, listened for two hours, prayed over my life, and then started rebuking Satan himself along with any other assigned demons that had been sent to kill me!

On our three hour drive back home, she blue-toothed her phone to the audio device of the car and played for me the preaching of a pastor who had preached to his congregation on how he struggled with severe depression and suicidal thoughts in the midst of his success. The pastor openly shared on how he immediately sought professional help in spite of his occupation as being a pastor. This got me through the rest of that day. Not long after that day, I sought the help that I needed to survive this ferocious attack on my life. It was at one of my therapy sessions that my counselor identified the abandonment I had experienced from my biological father at such an early age had plenty to do with what I had been struggling with now as an adult.

If it wasn't for my loving, caring, exquisite and spirit-tuned wife, and the help of *therapy*, I don't know if I would have made it far enough to write this book.

> *If the enemy can ISOLATE you, then he can ASSASSINATE you. —FF*

I learned during that season of my life *if the enemy can ISOLATE you, then he can ASSASSINATE you.*

> *It's hard to see past the problem when the problem is you. —FF*

It's hard to see past the problem when the problem is you.

I needed to do something that was going to make a change, something that would save my life and my church. I knew that if I couldn't INSPIRE my people then I would EXPIRE with my people. With the blessings of my inner circle, I took a three-month sabbatical for rest and to get help spiritually and professionally. I had no clue that the word *sabbatical* comes from the archaic word *sabbath*. All I needed

> *If I couldn't INSPIRE my people then I would EXPIRE with my people. —FF*

was rest, Jesus, and one book to read— the Bible. Set-backs are set-ups when you keep your head up.

> *Set-backs are set-ups when you keep your head up. —FF*

On my sabbatical I considered mistakes I may have made as a leader and pastor. It took me quite a while to actually believe that SOME things people say about me can be true. Rightly so, people are free to say what they would like and leave your life if they choose to.

On the other hand, I've learned that every time a negative word got back to me, I would judge myself, then ask a trusted and honest person if everything that was being said about me was true or not. At times, the person would be straightforward and at other times the person would say the issue was not my character.

I've now learned over the years that whenever I'm being criticized or talked about, I should be the very first one to take an inventory of my life. Why? Because *some of the stuff people say about you is really true.*

THE THREE-STEP ORDER TO CHECK YOURSELF

1. Honestly judge yourself of what is being said about you.
2. Ask your spouse or someone who you trust the most if they see character flaws of what you're being judged for.
3. If the character flaws are true, repent, ask for forgiveness from the person(s), and do your very best to change in those areas that need work.

Is it really true what people say about me?

Yes!—Some things are really true!

The spiritual gift of hater-ism

Our church previously had a rehab home that now we call the Thrive House; it's a twenty-four-hour sober living program that equips future leaders for ministry, callings, careers, and much more. Over the years, they have recorded three hip-hop albums. The first time that I had ever heard the word *hater-ism* was from a song on one of the albums. "Hater-ism" is an urban word that is defined as:

Haterism (Definition)—*A person that simply cannot be happy for another person's success. So rather than be happy, they make a point of exposing a flaw in that person.*

HERE IS THE TRUTH ABOUT HATER-ISM

1. Hater-ism is a disease.
2. One may catch it by just hating too much.
3. You will not notice your hating, even though it is painfully clear to everyone else around you.

HERE ARE THE SYMPTOMS OF HATER-ISM

1. Chronic hating.
2. Just being ignorant to anyone around you, for no reason.
3. Being a punk.
4. Not being able to back up what you say with any logical and/or sensible reason.
5. Hater-ism can be contagious like a virus.

Please go get your yearly hater exam. Haterism is serious, see your local Hateroligist for more information!

When Jesus was at the Feast of Tabernacles, a group of people started judging Him: ... *some of them said, "This man really is the Prophet." Others said, "He is the Christ." Still others said,*

"The Christ will not come from Galilee. The Scripture says that the Christ will come from David's family. And the Scripture says that the Christ will come from Bethlehem, the town where David lived." So, the people did not agree with each other about Jesus (**JOHN 7:40-43**).

Jesus was judged, hated, and made fun of His entire life as a human.

- **Jesus was judged as a child**—*His very own parents judged that at twelve years of age he was gone missing* **(Luke 2:39-52).**

- **Jesus was judged in His ministry**—*When Jesus came to the region of Caesarea Philippi, He asked His disciples, "Who do people say the Son of Man is?" They replied, "Some say John the Baptist; others say Elijah; and still others, Jeremiah or one of the prophets." "But what about you?" He asked. "Who do you say I am?" Simon Peter answered, "You are the Messiah, the Son of the living God." Jesus replied, "Blessed are you, Simon, son of Jonah, for this was not revealed to you by flesh and blood, but by my Father in heaven,"* **(MATTHEW 16:13-17).**

- **Jesus was judged when He died**—*One of the criminals who hung there hurled insults at Him: "Aren't you the Christ? Save yourself and us!"* **(LUKE 23: 39-41).**

- **Jesus was judged when He resurrected**—*Thomas in the Bible was absent one day when Jesus showed up after His resurrection to appear to the disciples. So, they told Him, "We have seen the Lord." But He said to them, "Unless I see in his hands the mark of the nails and place my finger into the mark of the nails, and place my hand into his side, I will never believe,"* **(JOHN 20:25).**

- **Jesus was judged when he ascended.** – *When Jesus was explaining that he was the bread of life, he then looked over at the disciples and they said: "This is very hard to understand. How can anyone accept it?" Jesus was aware that his disciples were complaining, so He said to them, "Does this offend you?"* (**JOHN 6:60-62**).

- **Jesus is still being judged today**—There are approximately 6.7 million Jewish people in the United States out of about 14 million worldwide that believe Jesus is the Messiah. The majority of the reason being cultural reasons.

In John chapter seven, judgement on Jesus is clearly seen. I am shown this when He challenged the teachers of the law, the Pharisees, and both groups thought they had a grand-slam case against Jesus. Both groups were self-righteously enslaved as many of us are today.

The teachers of the law and the Pharisees caught a woman in adultery red-handed and they had a proven case. For sure they thought they had a case that they would win when it came to "pointing the finger" at her. The problem with pointing fingers is that there are so

> *The problem with pointing fingers is that there are so many fingers covering your face, you don't see the log in your own eyes.* —FF

many fingers covering your face, you don't see the log in your own eyes.

They took possession of this adulterous woman and brought her into the temple. She had been caught! I can't imagine the fear, shame, and condemnation she must have been feeling that day. They forced the woman to stand before the people. They said to Jesus, "Teacher, this woman was caught having physical relations with a man who is not her husband. The law of Moses commands that we kill with stones every woman who does this. What do you say we should do?" They were asking this to trick Jesus so that they could have some charge against him. But Jesus knelt down and started writing on the ground with His finger. They continued to ask Jesus their question. So, He stood up and said, "Is there anyone here who has never sinned? The person without sin can throw the first stone at this woman." Then Jesus knelt down again and wrote on the ground. Those who heard Jesus began to leave one by one. The older men left first, and then the others. Jesus was left there alone with the woman. She was standing before Him. Jesus stood up again and asked her, "Woman, all of those people have gone. Has no one judged you guilty?" She answered, "No one has judged me, sir." Then Jesus said, "So I also don't judge you. You may go now."

> *The church house ought to be a place of healing, not killing. —FF*

41

1. **Haters**—Use their finger to condemn.

2. **Jesus**—Uses His finger to forgive.

The heartbreaking fact is that all this judging from the Pharisees takes place in the temple. It always amazes me how many people judge right there in the church house. The church house ought to be a place of healing, not killing.

> *I had to come to a place and realize that if Jesus loves me than I should love me too. —FF*

I had to come to a place and realize that if Jesus loves me than I should love me too. This is what Jesus was trying to get the adulterous woman to believe. If Jesus forgave her, then she should forgive herself.

As long as we don't let the praise go to our head and the judging to our heart, we'll be healed.

It took me quite a while to actually believe that SOME things people say about me are actually true. I guess where the deep hurt comes from is how I was willing to show continual love, receive people, look beyond others' shortcomings… and I assumed that people would do the same for me. *I was wrong!* Again, people are free to say what they would like, make their own decisions, and leave you if they choose to.

Let me give you a secret to a faster healing: Don't flirt with the hurt. I found that every time I would look back at the situation, I would just hurt more.

When I was a little boy, I remember my mom driving a car and my dad sitting in the passenger's seat. It was absolutely quiet and tense. I had no idea about what was happening or where we were going. We finally arrived at what I now know as the Ventura County Jail. My father got out of the car and headed toward the jail house. I cried *Dad! Dad!* He never looked back as he headed straight forward to turn himself in to jail. Now I know, he didn't want to flirt with the hurt.

> *Don't flirt with the hurt.*
> —FF

FRIENDLY FIRE!

"I'm sorry, I didn't mean to shoot you."

I n October 2003 at a New York Yankees game, one of my best pastor friends, and confidant, said to me in a conversation, *"Why do pastors talk bad about each other?"* Wow! What a great question he asked me that spring afternoon. We then began a pastor-to-pastor discussion. We couldn't understand why some pastors would talk behind our backs and then smile right to our faces at a church conference. We were both new pastors and I assumed we were growing in this area of friendly fire.

The conversation led us back, fixing our eyes on God and off of those *pulling the trigger.* At the end of our conversation he looked at me in my eyes and said, *"You know what Fernie? One day I'm going to preach a sermon titled 'Friendly Fire.'"* I don't know to this day if he ever did preach that sermon. He died not too far after that conversation.

Friendly Fire is an attack by neutral forces, while attempting to attack the enemy.

We hear of it all the time. Two kids are playing with real guns and one accidently shoots the other. It happens at war in a crossfire while engaging an enemy. It happens in the police force. Friendly Fire is accidental but still causes death. *"I'm sorry, I didn't mean to shoot you."*

I've never understood why people on the same team would attack one another, but as soon as I read the story of Gideon in the Bible, I realized why.

> *Friendly Fire is accidental but still causes death. —FF*

Gideon found himself fighting two armies against his one and only army. If we were to calculate the math in that battle, then this would mean that Gideon's army was outnumbered "five to one!"

Why was Gideon's army of just 300 men able to have the victory against two armies that totaled over 100,000 men? The answer can be found in one word— CONFUSION! Confusion will always get people to turn against one another. That's exactly what happened with the army that Gideon was fighting against. When Gideon's army had blown their ram horns and threw down the jars of

> *Confusion will always get people to turn against one another. —FF*

clay and shouted, the blaring sound caused 100,000 men to

enter into a state of confusion. The monstrous amount of men got so confused from the sound, they began to fight each other and eventually killed one another. I'm sure their intention wasn't to kill their own, but it was confusion that was the cause of *friendly fire*.

> *Satan knows that if he cannot kill, then his other tactic is to wound. —FF*

The defeated army either died or fled far away, never to be seen again. Satan knows that if he cannot kill, then his other tactic is to wound.

A bullet is so small, yet can kill an entire being, the tongue is so small, yet can kill an entire reputation.

> *A bullet is so small, yet can kill an entire being, the tongue is so small, yet can kill an entire reputation. —FF*

The average weight of the human tongue for adult males is 70 grams and for adult females 60 grams. This is just a little over 2 ounces. The human tongue also could never get tired like other muscles in our bodies can. It's amazing that just 60 grams can harm, ruin, and destroy.

This is scary: You can tame a tiger, but you can't tame a tongue—it's never been done. The tongue runs wild, a wanton killer. With our tongues we bless God our Father; with the same tongues we curse the very men and women He made in His image. Curses and blessings out of the same mouth! (**JAMES 3:8-10**).

Today, our tongues are the bullets in *friendly fire*. Some people are machine guns and others are single-shot pistols with their tongues... our tongues can produce up to ninety words in just one minute, but all it takes is just one to kill.

"GLOSSOLITIS"

"Glossolitis" is a serious medical condition that is marked by a swelling of the tongue.

In biblical terms, Glossolitis happens when the tongue is overused! Today, Glossolitis is known to be the most prevalent disease in the body of Christ and has the potential to destroy every person it infects. Gossip, in all its diabolic forms and manifestations, has become an epidemic in so many churches across the nation.

To make this plague worse, Christians have grown accustomed to its ways. We assume that it comes with the territory. "THIS ASSUMPTION IS OUR GREATEST PERIL."

Gossip is used in families, the workplace, high schools, and churches.

You may or may not have been a victim of this vicious disease, however, I advise you to take preventative measures and familiarize yourself with it. If you see anyone walking around with an overused tongue then get as far away as you can so you won't be infested with this *Diabolic* disease.

TONGUES OF FIRE
VS.
TOUNGUES OF LIARS

The tongue that is not controlled by the Holy Spirit is ready to strike, like a nervous and poisonous SNAKE!

TONGUES OF FIRE
A manifestation of the Holy Spirit.

When Paul placed his hands on them, the Holy Spirit came on them, and they spoke in tongues and prophesied **(ACTS 19:6)**.

Speaking in tongues should not be **dis.con.tinued** in the church! I don't believe that we should do away with tongues of fire. This power of the tongue is not one of the old school. This gift of speaking in tongues is a *manifestation* of the Holy Spirit, therefore, it should be *manifested* in the church. As a matter of fact, Paul's wishes for everyone in the church at Corinth: *"I would like every one of you to speak in tongues..."* **(1 Corinthians 14:5)**.

Scripture is not AGAINST speaking in tongues— only against the ABUSE of tongues.

TONGUES OF LIARS

A tongue that no man can tame.

A bit in the mouth of a horse controls the whole horse. A small rudder on a huge ship in the hands of a skilled captain sets a course in the face of the strongest winds. A word out of your mouth may seem of no account, but it can accomplish nearly anything— or destroy it! **(JAMES 3:3-5).**

The word *tame* means *"To domesticate, to subdue, bring under control."*

This word is describing how impossible it is to control the tongue without the help of the Holy Spirit. This is the exact same word that is used in Mark chapter five that talks of the demoniac: *Jesus and His disciples arrived on the other side of Lake Galilee, in the territory of Gerasa. As soon as Jesus got out of the boat, He was met by a man who came out of the burial caves there. This man had an evil spirit in him and lived among the tombs. Nobody could keep him tied with chains anymore; many times, his feet and his hands had been tied, but every time he broke the chains and smashed the irons on his feet. He was too strong for anyone to tame him. Day and night he wandered among the tombs and through the hills, screaming and cutting himself with stones* **(MARK 5:1-5).**

This same exact word was also used to describe the animal trainers who were experts at capturing and domesticating the wildest and most ferocious of beasts, such as lions, tigers, and bears. Normally, these animals would maul or kill a person, but these skilled trainers were able to take even the wildest animals and domesticate them—even turning them into house pets.

The fact that this word is used to describe the demoniac strongly suggests that the wild animal trainers had unsuccessfully attempted to subdue and *tame* the demoniac. This demoniac was so ferocious that those who could domesticate the most ferocious beasts were unable to subdue and *tame* this man.

TONGUES OF FIRE
A use for prayer

Speaking in tongues is speaking unto God. Therefore, it is prayer.

For one who speaks in a tongue does not speak to men but to God; for no one understands, but in his spirit he speaks mysteries **(1 Corinthians 14:2).**

Tongues of fire makes such a difference to prayer that Paul practiced it often in his life. *"I thank God I speak in tongues more than you all,"* **(1 Corinthians 14:18).** When we speak with *tongues of fire* in prayer, we don't understand that we are praying *the mind is unfruitful* but it is nevertheless "self-edifying" when you pray in tongues. When you speak your native tongue, or any language which you have consciously learned, your mind controls what is said. But speaking in tongues is a speaking forth prompted not by the *mind*, but by the *spirit*.

This is why Paul told the church, *"For if I pray in a tongue, my spirit prays, but my mind is unfruitful,"* (**1 Corinthians 14:14**). When I speak with tongues in fire, I don't decide what sound will come out next, I simply lift up my voice and *the spirit gives utterance.*

The Bible says that when we speak in tongues the "Spirit prays" and we "utter mysteries." I am praying with my spirit rather than with my mind.

You may say, Pastor Fernie, *"What blessing can it be to pray when you have no idea what you are praying about?"* Actually, this is one of its greatest blessings! The fact that your prayer is not subject to the limitations of your human intellect.

The mind...

- Has limited knowledge.
- Limited linguistic ability.
- Limited understanding.
- Can be prejudiced.

Tongues of fire is a God-appointed blessing that can bypass all the limitations of the intellectual mind.

Example;

A prayer with just the mind comes upward from the heart, and then must pass through the maze of our English language, theological, rational, emotional, and personal checkpoints before it is released upward. By the time it gets out, it can be just a trickle of prayer...

A prayer with tongues of fire comes upward from the depths, but instead of being channeled through the mind, it bypasses the mind and flows directly to God in a stream of spirit-prompted prayer!

TONGUES OF LIARS
A weapon of deadly poison

Just like the poisonous snake, venom is death-bearing. The tongue of a poisonous snake is depicted as an instrument that is full of death to its enemy.

It is...

Unruly

Unpredictable

Easily agitated

Ready to inject a load of deadly venom

In all likelihood one of the first *tongues of liars* we are introduced to in the Bible would be Moses' immediate family and his right-hand man. It's been said before that the people closest to you are the ones that can hurt you the most. Why is that? Because they are within reach to cause a more painful force.

Moses had married a Cushite woman, and Miriam and Aaron criticized him for it. They said, "Has the LORD spoken only through Moses? Hasn't He also spoken through us?" The LORD heard what they said **(Numbers 12:1-2)**.

We can see so clearly the deadly poison venting out from *tongues of liars. Here is the order of how it usually drips.*

1. **The first step: Talking behind a person's back and never giving them a chance to defend themselves.**

They both were not in agreement with Moses' decision to marry a Cushite woman. Moses' fiancé was not an Israelite, and obviously they didn't want her in the family.

It's funny how at times people who struggle with the *tongues of liars* make such a big issue of it when it's not even their problem. The sisters were not the ones who would marry this woman. Moses was going to marry her.

The sad thing about this sickening disease is that the victim is absent when he or she is being discussed, and is unable to defend themselves or even offer an explanation.

After many years being a pastor, I eventually began getting nervous every time someone would tell me *"I got your back."* I would think in my mind, *Of course you do, it's easier to stab.* Aaron went from holding up Moses' hands to tying up his hands.

> *Aaron went from holding up Moses' hands to tying up his hands. —FF*

2. **The second step: Like an infection, it begins to spread and infects others.**

They both move from talking about Moses' marriage to questioning his leadership.

They said, "Has the LORD spoken only through Moses? Hasn't He also spoken through us?" The LORD heard what they said (**Numbers 12:2**).

Aaron and Miriam's names are given as leaders for the Israelites in Micah chapter six.

I brought you out of Egypt; I rescued you from slavery; I sent Moses, Aaron, and Miriam to lead you (**Micah 6:4**).

What the two needed to understand is that they might have been leaders, but they were NOT Moses' leader. God appointed Moses as leader of the Israelites, however, people whose tongues are out of control can't help but to encroach as if they are the final authority.

3. **The third step: It leads to the destruction and death of the victim's character.**

This is *friendly fire* at its best. Even if gossip begins in innocence, it quickly becomes malicious. After all the damage and death caused is when they say, *"I'm sorry, I didn't mean to shoot you."*

I think one of the biggest mistakes that a person makes that has this disease is they don't realize that God is hearing their entire conversation. The victim may not be present, but God is always present.

After Aaron and Miriam had all they had to say... Numbers 12:2 says:... *AND THE LORD HEARD IT!* Not only did the Lord hear it, but He informed Moses of Aaron and Miriam's conversation:

... immediately the LORD called to Moses, Aaron, and Miriam and said, "Go out to the Tabernacle, all three of you!" And the three of them went out. Then the LORD descended in the pillar of cloud and stood at the entrance of the Tabernacle. "Aaron and Miriam!" He called, and they stepped forward. And the LORD said to them, "Now listen to me! Even with prophets, I the LORD communicate by visions and dreams. But that is not how I communicate with my servant Moses. He is entrusted with my entire house. I speak to him face to face, directly, and not in riddles! He sees the LORD as he is. Should you not be afraid to criticize him?" The LORD was furious with them, and He departed. As the cloud moved from above the Tabernacle, Miriam suddenly became white as snow with leprosy. When Aaron saw what had happened, he cried out to Moses, "Oh, my Lord! Please don't punish us for this sin we have so foolishly committed," (**Numbers 12:4-11**).

There are seven things the Lord hates, and one of the seven is *a lying tongue* (**Proverbs 6:16,17**).

TONGUES OF FIRE
A use for twenty-four hours a day

Jesus never gave us just one way to pray. I believe that there are so many different ways to pray:

Sitting

Standing

Walking

Bowing

Kneeling

Although Jesus never gave us just one way to pray, the Bible does instruct us *always* to pray in 1 Thessalonians 5:17. We are instructed to pray continually

One of the blessings with *tongues of fire* is that you're able to do it at times and in situations where normal prayer, requiring heightened concentration, would be impossible. It's like putting up an invisible shield around you with the ability to screen out all foul attacks from the enemy. Since this is a prayer directly upward to God and a language that only God can understand, the enemy is thrown into confusion when you begin to speak in tongues since he does not understand such a language.

I've found that every time I am done speaking in tongues, I come out of prayer feeling refreshed and invigorated, and ready to face anything that comes my way.

TONGUES OF LIARS
An intricate form of diabolic behavior

Four patterns to diagnose if you have *tongues of liars*.

1. You cannot keep a secret.

A gossip goes around revealing a secret, but the trustworthy keeps a confidence **(Proverbs 11:13).**

The danger of gossipers is that they appear to be our trustworthy friends. What's sad is that you and I feel a sense of relief after sharing our heart, we actually feel encouraged that God placed a person in our life to share our burdens with. Then the feelings of relief or comfort are quickly replaced with dismay when we discover that the gossiper has spread our private heart to others!

2. You get your significance from the victim's pain.

A gossip's words are like eating cheap candy; do you really want junk like that in your belly? **(Proverbs 18:8).**

The tragic fact of a habitual gossiper is that he develops a sense of superiority at burying others with their words. The gossiper simulates compassion when they hear you out. The gossiper might even shed a tear while you're talking. But as soon as you're gone they begin to search their mental files of lists of people who might be interested in your private matter!

Without wood, fire goes out; without gossip conflict dies down **(Proverbs 26:20).**

Once the gossiper breaks the big story—the rush he feels becomes an addiction. The worst symptom of a gossiper is parallel to the symptoms of a drug addict. He doesn't see himself as a gossiper; as a matter of fact, he gets offended if you label him as one too. The simple fact is, he has a huge need to light the fires of gossip because when the flame dies down, HE NEEDS HIS NEXT FIX.

3.   You have an enemy's knife in a friendly hand.

Your enemy shakes hands and greets you like an old friend, all the while conniving against you. When he speaks warmly to you, don't believe him for a minute; he's just waiting for the chance to rip you off. No matter how cunningly he conceals his malice, eventually his evil will be exposed in public **(Proverbs 26:24-26).**

FRIENDLY FIRE!

A fundamental principle: "No one can hurt your feelings without your permission." We must remember that we are in a war. You can't call yourself a WARrior if you've never fought in a WAR. There will be casualties, however, it's worse when they are caused by *"friendly fire." Sorry, I didn't mean to shoot you.*

> *You can't call yourself a WARrior if you've never fought in a WAR. —FF*

CHAPTER FOUR

BUT ALL I HAVE LEFT IS...

"Really? You want my very last drop of blood?"

I've been fortunate enough to be in the locker room plenty of times with professional boxer ***Fernando Vargas***. He is the youngest boxer in history to win a light middleweight world title at the young age of just twenty-one. He took his career to the heights of being a three-time world champion and the boxing world knows him as ***"El Feroz," "The Aztec Warrior,"*** **and** ***"Ferocious Fernando Vargas."*** His professional boxing record totals at thirty-one fights, twenty-six wins, and just five losses. Twenty-two of his wins were by way of knockout!

He remembers the first day he walked into my church office, and I remember the first day I walked into his office (The ring in Las Vegas, Nevada).

The first time I did the *ring walk* with him, I couldn't believe what I was seeing, hearing, and *feeling!*

Every single time, right before he was called to leave the locker room for the main event of the evening, he ALWAYS made it a point for prayer. He would kneel, I would place my right hand over his forehead, and sometimes even the entire team would gather in a circle holding hands while I said the prayer.

"Lord Jesus, I ask that you protect Fernando tonight as he steps in that ring. As he puts his life on the line, I ask that YOU would be his guard, his strength, his wisdom, and his purpose for this fight. Lord Jesus, I also ask that you protect the man on the opposite side of the ring too, but I do ask that you will also allow Fernando to knock him out IN THE NAME OF JESUS CHRIST!—AMEN."

We then would leave the locker room together and make that infamous live televised pay-per-view *ring walk* with millions watching around the world and over 21,000 roaring fans standing and cheering, high-fiving, and making vanquishing comments. Playing over the arena's enormous sound system would be the same song he always walked out to: *"No Me Se Rajar"* **(I don't know how to give up)** by the Mexican cultural icon, *Vicente Fernandez.* The lyrics in English translate: *"To me you don't scare me, big tongue guys. You just conceit to overwhelm. I am not that kind of man. I am not afraid of nothing and even when I am lost. I don't know to give up."*

At times, God answered our prayer and other times he didn't.

During this season of Fernando's career, I learned that just because someone loses doesn't mean they're a loser. You can still be a world champion with some losses on your record.

I'm reminded of a scripture that seems to be tucked away very well in the Bible:

> *You can still be a world champion with some losses on your record.* —FF

Amos 3:12

This is what the Lord says: "Just as a shepherd might save from the lion's mouth only two leg bones or a scrap of an ear, the Israelis will be saved in a similar manner..."

So many people let this book pass them up as they read through their Bible. It's written from the minor prophet Amos. He confronts what Matthew Henry's commentary calls *"a stupid, senseless, heedless people."* Sins that were found among them, by which God was provoked. God wanted them repented and reformed.

Amos predicts that they shall be in the hands of the enemy—as a lamb is in the mouth of a lion—all devoured and eaten up, and they shall be utterly unable to make a resistance. And for those who manage to escape and survive, they will with just *two legs, or shanks, of a lamb, or, a piece of an ear*, which the lion drops, or the shepherd takes from him!

The book you are reading is titled **dis.con.tinued.** If I were a witness in that crowd watching the lion devour a sheep, I would certainly think that it was over for that sheep. A couple of leg bones sticking out, a piece of an ear falling from the jaws of a lion! Yup... **dis.con.tinued** is what I would have likely said.

I bet there are multiple readers right now saying, *That's exactly how I feel! I AM that sheep. I have nothing left.* NO husband, NO job, NO title, NO money, NO pastor, NO FUTURE! Your feelings may be correct, but you are the sheep—He is the shepherd.

> *God doesn't see what you have lost, He sees what you have left. —FF*

Obviously, the shepherd still sees some *value* in you. You may not see it, and the people who have declared you **dis.con. tinued** may not see your value—but God doesn't see what you have lost, He sees what you have left. In God's eyes, two legs and a piece of an ear is worth the battle for you against a lion that has you lock-jawed in his mouth. You are not finished nor cancelled. You are redeemable!

> *A piece of an "ear" and two "legs" are still enough to continue to "walk" in what you have "heard." —FF*

A piece of an *"ear"* and two *"legs"* are still enough to continue to *"walk"* in what you have *"heard."*

It's never too late, no matter how expired you feel.

Ask Sarah and Abraham who thought it was too late for them to have Isaac, ask Hannah who thought she would never have a baby despite a closed womb. You are never EXPIRED! As long as you have an ear to hear and two legs to walk. All the blood may have been sucked out of you has left you powerless but remember *the blood of Jesus* never loses its power.

It's pretty amazing when life seems to crumble as it does in the lion's mouth, and how the natural reflex is always the same:

> *You are never EXPIRED! As long as you have an ear to hear and two legs to walk. All the blood may have been sucked out of you has left you powerless but remember the blood of Jesus never loses its power. —FF*

ANXIETY—STRESS—WORRY!

I can't lie! I'm one of the 70% of pastors that fights depression. In Luke chapter 22:39-45 we get an outstanding picture of when *anxiety—stress—and worry* hits an individual. This passage is one of the few times we find Jesus at His lowest. The Bible paints a graphic atmosphere in Jesus' life as He faces what so many confront today.

[39] Then, accompanied by the disciples, He left the upstairs room and went as usual to the Mount of Olives. [40] There He told them, "Pray God that you will not be overcome by temptation."

[41-42] *He walked away, perhaps a stone's throw, and knelt down and prayed this prayer: "Father, if you are willing, please take away this cup of horror from me. But I want your will, not mine."* [43] *Then an angel from heaven appeared and strengthened Him,* [44] *for He was in such agony of spirit that He broke into a sweat of blood, with great drops falling to the ground as He prayed more and more earnestly.* [45] *At last He stood up again and returned to the disciples—only to find them asleep, exhausted from grief* **(Luke 22:39-45).**

ANXIETY, STRESS, AND WORRY HITS DURING MONUMENTAL LIFE EXPERIENCES.

It's amazing how HIGH a person can be in life, yet so LOW. It was on a mountaintop where Jesus called His prayer a *"cup of horror."*

> *It was on a mountaintop where Jesus called His prayer a "cup of horror. —FF*

"Father, if you are willing, please take away this cup of horror from me," **(LUKE 22:42).**

It's during *monumental life* experiences when we are tempted to fall into a vicious state of anxiety, stress, and worry:

- **The death of a loved one**
- **A big purchase**
- **A decision concerning your future**
- **Mid-life crisis**

- **The peak of a marriage**
- **A bad doctor's report**
- **A newborn recently added to your family**

It doesn't surprise me that Mark calls this moment the *"awful hour."* It's this hour that will *steal your sleep, put knots in your stomach, and dominate your thinking.* I love what Isaiah the prophet says concerning our results of Jesus' awful hour:

When He sees all that is accomplished by His anguish, He will be satisfied. And because of His experience, my righteous servant will make it possible for many to be counted righteous, for He will bear all their sins **(Isaiah 53:11)**.

Jesus said, don't worry about tomorrow because tomorrow has enough worry of its own. Worry has enough weight standing alone, so why take it upon ourselves to carry around the extra weight? We are told that the *weight* of the world will be on His shoulders. Why not let Him carry the weight of anxiety, stress, and worry? He is a lot stronger than us.

ANXIETY, STRESS, AND WORRY HITS WHEN WE WANT CONTROL

Control is power that influences or directs an individual's behavior or their course of events. *Anxiety, stress, and worry* don't come from thinking about the future, but by trying to control the future. Jesus said the same thing three times in his prayer in Mark 14:35: *"Get me out of this. Take this cup away from me."* We are able to see the humanity of Christ in his moment of desperation when his father needed to send an angel to take care of Jesus' needs. When Jesus was tempted in the wilderness, His father didn't *take Him out of it,* but walked Him *through* it.

> *Anxiety, stress, and worry don't come from thinking about the future, but by trying to control the future. —FF*

My brother-in-law recently returned from the beautiful redwoods in northern California where you will find the tallest trees on earth. As he was zip-lining through this park, his guide started to tell him a little more about these trees.

> *When Jesus was tempted in the wilderness, His father didn't take Him out of it, but walked Him through it. —FF*

Redwood trees are...

- The largest living things on earth.
- Grow up to 380 feet tall.
- Create the strength to withstand powerful winds and floods by extending their roots more than 50 feet from the trunk and living in groves where their roots can intertwine.

- Have been around for about 240 million years and in California for at least 20 million years.
- Capture more carbon dioxide (CO_2) from our cars, trucks, and power plants than any other tree on earth.
- As the climate changes, the redwood forests in the Santa Cruz Mountains are one of very few places that can provide a refuge for plants and animals to survive, because the area has many microclimates, is cooled by coastal summertime fog, and is still largely unpaved.
- Redwoods live so long and are treasured by humans for building because they are extremely resistant to insects, fire, and rot. There was a point in time when San Francisco's building codes required redwood lumber to be used in the foundations of new structures. A redwood's bark can be one foot thick, and it contains tannin which protects the tree from fire, insects, fungus, and diseases.

Here is a solution to anxiety, stress, and worry. A steady flow of problems demands a constant flow of prayers.

> *A steady flow of problems demands a constant flow of prayers.—FF*

1. **Spend more time with God.**

    Notice that Jesus took three men with Him up the mountain. And though He talked to them about

His anxiety, stress, and worry, He spent more time talking to God about the subject. Our mistake is that we tend to do the opposite. We spend more time talking to men about our problems than we do talking to God.

2. **Remember, it's just a cup.**

Although the cup was one of horror, it was just a cup. He didn't ask his father to remove the ocean, river, or lake of suffering. He called it a cup of suffering. We can see the bottom of a cup but we can't see the bottom of an ocean!

> *We can see the bottom of a cup but we can't see the bottom of an ocean! —FF*

We worry so much about the future that God already has in His control. He has your past, present, and future in His hands.

THE DASH LIFE

The word *expired* is not just another word for **dis.con. tinued**, but it's also another word for a date of death on obituaries. Death will come, but it hasn't arrived yet. However, what you are facing now is what I call a "dash life." And the dash life usually is something lonely, painful, confusing, and costly.

If you notice that when someone dies, you'll find on their headstone the "dash." *What's the dash?* It's the space of time from which you were born until the time you died.

As weird as it may sound, every time I've walked through a cemetery, I've always looked at the *"dash"* and said to myself, *I wonder how this person lived their life during the dash?*

> *If you notice that when someone dies, you'll find on their headstone the "dash." What's the dash? It's the space of time from which you were born until the time you died.—FF*

When I die, my headstone will say 1970 - ? John writes of what Jesus says concerning his identity: *I am the Alpha and the Omega, the First and the Last, the Beginning and the End* **(REVELATION 22:13)**.

If HE is the first and the last, then EVERYTHING that happens "IN THE DASH" does not go UNFORESEEN.

Michael Jordan

A few years ago, my wife gave me a birthday gift of a golf tee time in Santa Barbara, California. While I was enjoying my present, I noticed a very familiar face that left no doubt in my mind that it was NBA STAR MICHAEL JORDAN. I walked up to him and asked if I could take a picture with him. *Michal Jordan...* the greatest basketball player of all time! Jordan was one of the most effectively marketed athletes of his generation. In 1999, he was named the greatest North American athlete of the 20th century by ESPN. Jordan was inducted into the Basketball Hall of Fame in 2009—an athlete that deserved the upmost honor and respect as a professional basketball player.

So I saw him in person and got a picture with him. I've seen the highlights of his career. But what I DIDN'T SEE, along with millions of others, was what his life was like *before* he became a multi-million dollar basketball player.

We didn't see him living in Brooklyn, NY, trying out for the baseball team and football teams in high school. We weren't in attendance when he tried out for the varsity basketball team during his sophomore year which, at just 5'11", he was deemed too short to play at that level.

You and I may not have been there that day, but his *taller* friend (Harvest Smith) was. Harvest and Michael tried out together; his friend made the team, but Michael didn't.

I would assume years later, Harvest Smith nearly fainted with amazement when he saw his shorter friend become the greatest basketball player of all time and rise on a pedestal as the WORLD CLASS athlete that the entire world wanted to be a part of.

The point I'm trying to make with this illustration is that EVERYBODY applauses the accomplishments in a star's life but don't necessarily realize what happened during the *dash* it took to get there.

ALPHA = The first letter in the GREEK alphabet.
OMEGA = The last letter in the GREEK alphabet.

God is the MASTER at what happens in *the dash!* Often we can sit in a church service hearing inspirational, anointed, visionary sermons and dream big about our future, what we want to become, about the finished product of our life.

Successful people usually are not "born stars." It's "SCARS" that make them "STARS."

When you exited the womb of your mother, you were not the weight and height you are today.

> *Successful people usually are not "born stars." It's "SCARS" that make them "STARS."—FF*

We all were born SMALL. Every successful organization began small:

- Disneyland began with a mouse.
- Amazon began with a VHS tape.
- Pizza Hut began with a small red brick building.
- McDonalds began with two brothers.
- Ringling Bros., Barnum & Bailey Circus which later on went to be known as "The Greatest Show on Earth" began with one African Elephant, named "Old Bet."

God was so correct when he said to Job one day:

Then what you had in the past will seem small compared with the great prosperity you'll have in the future (**Job 8:7**).

Zacchaeus had to be SMALL before Jesus would make him BIG. Everyone in that crowd that day only saw JESUS looking UP to this SHORT and SMALL man on a tree, but nobody realized this was part of his *dash life* before he would have Jesus spend the night at his house.

> *"You might not be where you WANT to be but thank God you're not where you USED to be."*

"You might not be where you WANT to be but thank God you're not where you USED to be."

King David—WASN'T ALWAYS A KING

Paul—WASN'T ALWAYS THE APOSTLE

Moses—WASN'T ALWAYS THE LEADER

Peter—WASN'T ALWAYS THE CHIEF

Gideon—WASN'T ALWAYS THAT MIGHTY MAN OF VALOR

Joseph—WASN'T' ALWAYS "FAVORED"

Barabbas—WASN'T ALWAYS THE FORTUNATE

Deborah—WASN'T AWLAYS A JUDGE

Esther—WASN'T ALWAYS A QUEEN

Judas—WASN'T ALWAYS "THE TRAITOR"

With the exception of Judas, they all made it through the *dash life* limping with just a piece of an ear and surviving the mighty jaws of a lion… and so can you!

King David

We see him today as a king, but his humble beginnings were just a sling.

When David was out in the back sheep-tending, his brothers were out front pre-tending.

In the midst of David's *dash life*, he wrote these lyrics:

> *We see him today as a king, but his humble beginnings were just a sling. When David was out in the back sheep-tending, his brothers were out front pre-tending. —FF*

"*He reached down from on high and took hold of me; he drew me out of deep waters. He rescued me from my powerful enemy, from my foes, who were too strong for me. They confronted me in the day of my disaster, but the Lord was my support. He brought me out into a spacious place; He rescued me because He delighted in me,*" **(Psalm 18:16-19)**.

As a child, since David was the youngest, he never had the privilege to lead any of his siblings. He only *followed* his entire youth! He had no one younger to wrestle and win by way of submission hold. All seven of his brothers were stronger, more experienced, and (of course) older than him.

> *Although David was often alone in the field he really wasn't. He always carried slings and strings. —FF*

Although David was often alone in the field he really wasn't. He always carried slings and strings. Everywhere he went he had those two small beginnings that would eventually take him to his throne. I imagine that if it were not for his slings and strings, he could have died of loneliness—especially when he knew that the prophet Samuel was in his father's living room selecting from all of his older *pretending* brothers. Pretending that they were qualified to be a king. However, we would later learn that it isn't a title that makes a man a leader, but his ability do the work of a leader before being called one. When it was time to do the work of a leader, none of David's brothers wanted to even look at Goliath for any longer than sixty seconds, while all it took was sixty seconds for David to defeat the giant.

It was in that house where we found out that God does not look at what man looks at. We judge a person by the way they look and sound; God judges a person by their sound living. Being that David was the only one out back with the sheep, he was introduced to something called *loneliness* that he would later in life know how to cope with. As a young boy I'm sure he cried as he was the *only one* in the back, being shelved for a later use. And as he sat all alone he would often

> *It was in that house where we found out that God does not look at what man looks at. We judge a person by the way they look and sound; God judges a person by their sound living.—FF*

take out his stringed guitar, that his brothers called a joke, and his sling, that his brothers called a toy. David would then *strum, cry,* and *write* because that's what writers do. They cry with the overwhelming anointing that rests on them with a pen and paper.

It didn't matter if anyone was around to praise David's songs, although today they would easily get the attention they deserve: "Elevation Worship," "Bethel," and "Mosaic MSC." His voice could have made it to the top three on the music charts. He knew that his *latter* would be greater than his *present.* His mourning will turn into dan*SING* and his weeping will turn into joy. The challenge is when the Bible says that weeping may endure for

> *And as he sat all alone he would often take out his stringed guitar, that his brothers called a joke, and his sling, that his brothers called a toy. —FF*

a night, but joy would come in the morning—it never said what morning!

I'm sure David wasn't surprised that his audience of ONE (God) would later in life attract an audience of an entire nation, and eventually the entire globe. David's humble beginnings called him to sing and play to poor sheep, to then play in a

> *The challenge is when the Bible says that weeping may endure for a night, but joy would come in the morning—it never said what morning! —FF*

palace full of riches! God was teaching David to give it his all to a sheep who wouldn't understand nor possibly appreciate his music, because he was learning that whatever he did, he would do it all for the honor and glory of God.

Those people that announced you as **dis.con.tinued** are making #1 songs out of you. David's *dash life* moments were teaching him that... *"HE HAD TO SERVE A KING BEFORE HE WOULD BE MADE ONE HIMSELF!"*

David wasn't only a SINGER, he was a SLINGER. He was singing while slinging.

Like Tiger Woods, the accuracy of his swings were eventually able to tell the golf ball which way he wanted them to fly. In the sport of golfing, this is what we call *shaping your shots*. David learned how to shape his shots.

> *Those people that announced you as dis.con.tinued are making #1 songs out of you.* —FF

After God trusted him with sheep, He trusted him with bears, giants, and eventually position. Most people see leadership backwards: they want a position first, and the battles second. David was finding out that the *dash life* was something extraordinary! Everything he was going through would serve to bring God ALL the glory.

> *David found out that, "WHEN GOD CRUSHES a man GOD is BREAKING the man; when SAUL is CRUSHING a man SAUL is DESTROYING that man!"* —FF

David found out that, "WHEN GOD CRUSHES a man GOD is BREAKING the man; when SAUL is CRUSHING a man SAUL is DESTROYING that man!"

Don't believe that you can't do much with just two legs and a piece of an ear. All David had was a sling and strings! Little do people know that it's a small sling that will raise a big king.

> *Little do people know that it's a small sling that will raise a big king. —FF*

Let the people call you dis.con.tinued, but like David, you'll go from CAVES into CASTLES! Diamonds are processed before they are displayed. Don't worry about your future and always remember that a boomerang returns with greater of a force than it had when leaving the master's hand.

> *Let the people call you dis.con.tinued, but like David, you'll go from CAVES into CASTLES! —FF*

CHAPTER FIVE

THE ONLY TIME YOU SHOULD LOOK DOWN AT SOMEONE

*"Why kick a man when he's down
and use him while he's up."*

When Dr. Martin Luther King Jr. was shot, Jesse Jackson was in the parking lot one floor below. Jackson told reporters he was the last person to speak to him, and that Dr. Martin Luther King Jr. died in his arms.

Jesse Jackson was born to his mother, Helen Burns, and father, Noah Louis Robinson, *a former professional boxer* (which explains the **DNA** of the fighter Jesse Jackson would later go on to become in life).

As a young child, Jackson was taunted by other children about his out-of-wedlock birth and has stated that those experiences helped motivate him to succeed.

It's a lot easier to now understand why he came up with the saying: *The only time you should look down at someone is when you are helping them up.*

Jackson attended the racially segregated *Sterling High School* in Greenville, where he was elected student class president, finished tenth in his class, and earned letters in baseball, football, and basketball. Upon graduating from high school in 1959, he rejected a contract from a minor league professional baseball team so that he could attend the University of Illinois on a football scholarship.

At A&T, Jackson played quarterback and was elected student body president. He became active in local civil rights protests against segregated libraries, theaters, and restaurants. He graduated with a B.S. in sociology in 1964, then attended the Chicago Theological Seminary on a scholarship.

He dropped out in 1966, three classes short of earning his master's degree, to focus full-time on the Civil Rights Movement. He was ordained a minister in 1968, and *in 2000 was awarded a Master of Divinity Degree* based on his previous credits earned plus his life experience and subsequent work.

I would assume that the man who said, ***The only time you should look down at someone is when you are helping them up*** was worthy of having been awarded by President Clinton **"The Presidential Medal of Freedom,"** the nation's *highest honor* bestowed on civilians in August 2000.

The first time I read that quote in my life, the power of it dropped me to my seat!

I remember the first book I attempted to publish was titled *Let's get ready to HUMBLE.* It was a book about how people won battles through humility. I believe humility is one of the greatest attractions to God.

One day Jesus entered and walked through Jericho. There was a man there, his name Zacchaeus, the head tax man and quite rich. He wanted desperately to see Jesus, but the crowd was in his way—he was a short man and couldn't see over the crowd. So, he ran on ahead and climbed up in a sycamore tree, so he could see Jesus when he came by (LUKE 19:1-4).

The name of this chapter is the total opposite of what Jesus did. He didn't look down on people, He looked *up* to them. Zacchaeus was a short man that couldn't be seen behind or in front of everyone else. Everyone else was taller, had more gifts, were better looking... perhaps more qualified, in a way. His only solution would be to climb a tree on his own, although he was wealthy enough to pay someone to raise him up, he wave his hands, and made some noise to get the attention of Jesus. *It worked! Humility always does.*

When Jesus got to the tree, *He looked up* and said, "Zacchaeus, hurry down. Today is my day to be a guest in your home." Zacchaeus scrambled out of the tree, hardly believing his good luck, delighted to take Jesus home with him. Jesus LOOKS UP to little people.

> *Jesus LOOKS UP to little people. —FF*

I have always been amazed with the people that have all the odds stacked against them but have proven to an entire world that it's not about the obstacles they're facing, it's about the God that is for them.

I remember when I invited **Nick Vujicic** to my church to plant seeds for a revival in Ventura County. Almost everyone knows of Nick Vujicic, but just in case you don't, I'll provide a little background. Nick was born in Melbourne, Australia, in 1982 without fully formed limbs. According to his autobiography, his mother refused to see him or hold him when the nurse held him in front of her, but she and her husband eventually accepted the condition and understood it as "God's plan for their son." *Nick attempted suicide but notes that he had an amazingly normal childhood.*

> *I have always been amazed with the people that have all the odds stacked against them but have proven to an entire world that it's not about the obstacles they're facing, it's about the God that is for them. —FF*

Originally, he was born with the toes of his foot fused. An operation was performed to separate the toes so that he could use them as fingers to grab, turn a page, or do other things. He has been able to use his foot to operate an electric wheelchair, a computer, and a mobile phone.

He thrived in his teenage and young adult years despite being bullied. After his mother showed him a newspaper article about a man dealing with a severe disability when he was seventeen, he started to give talks at his prayer group.

Nick graduated from Griffith University at the age of twenty-one with a Bachelor of Commerce degree, as well as a double major in accountancy and financial planning. He can golf, swim, and do so much more than people who have all of their limbs can do. But what he does best is WINS SOULS AROUND THE WORLD!

Why is it that we kick a man when he's down and use him while he's up? We should never kick a man while he is down, let alone look down on him when he feels he hit rock-bottom. How many homeless people do you just walk by? I am not asking how many of them you walk by and don't give money to, I am asking how many you walk by and don't say hi to? A two-letter word like *Hi* can carry more value that two hundred-dollar bills.

How do you imagine the little boy who was kicked to the curb amongst all the big dogs when Jesus asked for food and one of the disciples— Andrew, brother to Simon Peter— said, *"There's a little boy here who has five barley loaves and two fish. But that's a drop in the bucket for a crowd like this."* How would you like to be called a drop in the bucket? This is what's called being kicked NOT while you are down but KICKED DOWN while you are standing. That's even worse!

Israel Houghton, while talking on the Chad Veach podcast (Leadership Lean in), expresses his thoughts on getting back up when kicked down. He states that if he has approximately 436 comments on a social media post and 431 of them are positive, and five are negative why would we pay attention to those five and bypass the 431 that are applauding?? What's in our scientific make-up that only draws us to the negative? Chad Veach asks Israel why is it, in the circle of Christianity, we love for our own to remain down after they fall? Why in Christianity are we driven to win the lost, but we struggle to reach the found? Why would we shoot our wounded and carve them up? Why do we proudly lift our heroes up—and when they fall, we jump all over them? Chad makes a good point on this podcast.

> *Why do we proudly lift our heroes up—and when they fall, we jump all over them?*

Not only has *Israel Houghton* been on nearly every platform at conferences around the world, but more importantly, has been in every green room. Israel says those green rooms are very, very interesting! It is a case study to him nowadays. He could remember how many of those green rooms he walked out of because there were so many captains of the industry scouring their peers. He's like, *I don't want to be a part of this conversation.*

Later on in his own career, Israel Houghton goes through his cup of life: a divorce and all his personal stuff and he had friends call him saying, *Israel, They were murdering you in the green room tonight!*

Israel said that in his career he never wanted to participate in that kind of stuff and now he's the subject of it. Why do we do that? *Why do we kick people when they're down and use them while they're up?* The more we do that the more our circle is going to shrink. The people that are looking at us that have any kind of clue or ethics are looking at the body of Christ and saying, *If you guys are doing that to each other then why would I want to join?*

What is it about the insecure soul that wants to see someone lose in life and are secretly thrilled when someone falls? Unfortunately, there are too many of us that celebrate the people falling, than picking up the phone and doing some calling.

> *Unfortunately, there are too many of us that celebrate the people falling, than picking up the phone and doing some calling. —FF*

Instead of putting our two hands together to clap we ought to put our two hands together to pray. Pray for their family, their spouse, their ministry, their business, their reputation, their sanity.

> *Instead of putting our two hands together to clap we ought to put our two hands together to pray. —FF*

I remember one day on the other side of the tracks where I was raised. One of my best friends had gotten jumped (beat up) by three other guys on the side yard of my house. My friend had no chance for any offense fighting, let alone defense. The following day, his older brothers returned to my neighborhood looking for the guys who beat their little brother. I tagged along with them to help find the guys. When we found them, one of them ran as fast as a cheetah down my block, and when he was caught, fists were released with fury as hard as my friend's older brothers can punch! This guy was not only bloody but was left unconscious on the pavement under a diesel truck. My friend's older brother walked away with his fists dripping with blood, then made a 180 degree turn and walked back with a murderous spirit to the unconscious lifeless body—and with full force kicked him as hard as any man could! What I heard next was every ounce of wind that was reserved in that lifeless body exit with such a sound that his own mother would have fainted from fear.

At that moment I said to myself, *What's the point in kicking a man while he's down?*

I know what it feels like to be kicked while I am down, and you probably do too! I don't understand it, even if it was deserved, but I go especially crazy when it happens and you did nothing to deserve it.

I believe we are living in the last days. We are the generation who have become lovers of themselves. Paul said it well in 2 Timothy.

But mark this: There will be terrible times in the last days. People will be lovers of themselves, lovers of money, boastful, proud, abusive, disobedient to their parents, ungrateful, unholy, (2 **Timothy 3:1-2**).

> *For some people, the only way to lift themselves up is to pull someone down.* —FF

For some people, the only way to lift themselves up is to pull someone down.

We are living in a time that has been prophesied long ago. If you don't believe it, just take a look at everyone's social media platforms. You'll find they all have one thing in common... **#SELFIES**.

The United States Department of Transportation estimated that during 2014, the so-called **"Year of the Selfie,"** 33,000 people taking selfies while driving were injured. Think about how popular selfies have become. There is a millionaire out there somewhere that invented the "Selfie Stick":

It is reported that selfies now cause more deaths worldwide than shark attacks.

Last year over 54 deaths in India alone were by way of selfies.

Out of all deaths that occur by way of selfies, 75% of the victims are men, and the average age is under 21-years-old.

Why would 75% of the victims be guys? Because guys do stupid stuff!

Selfie Death #1

October 15, 2011 (U.S.) Three teenagers (two sisters and a friend) were killed by a train while posing for a selfie, which was visible on the final picture they posted to Facebook. The caption read; *"Standing right by a train ahaha this is awesome!!!!"*

Selfie Death #2

July 1, 2017 four college students at the Federal University of Technology were taking selfies in a canoe while boating on a campus pond. The canoe capsized. Two of them drowned.

Selfie Death #3

A 19-year-old from Texas died of a single gunshot wound to the throat after accidentally pulling the trigger of a gun, but for some reason thinking he was snapping the photo button on his phone.

The challenge that we face at times isn't always what people say about us that gets us down, it's what we say about *ourselves* that gets us there.

Don't let anyone look down on you because you are young, but set an example for the believers in speech, in conduct, in love, in faith and in purity (**1 Timothy 4:12**).

It was *Jesse Jackson* that said, "The only time you should look down at someone is when you are helping them up." I'll say, "**The only time you should look down at yourself is when you are helping you up.**"

When a young thin, beardless David kneels down by the stream to choose his stones to place in his sack for the battle against Goliath, instead of analyzing his features in the reflection of the water, he *"reaches past himself."* The ripple effect in the water gave a distorted image of who David really was (the same effect found in carnival mirrors). What we see in the mirror will reflect how we act as a person. Self-image determines our behavior. Mirrors don't tell the truth because they don't show what's on the inside.

> *Mirrors don't tell the truth because they don't show what's on the inside.*

It's not so much about the us who we see in the mirror, it's who's standing "WITH US" next to the mirror.

Goliath saw David as a nobody, just a little skinny kid that apparently was not a threat whatsoever. He attempted to intimidate David with these words: "Am I a dog that you come at me with sticks?"

> *It's not so much about the us who we see in the mirror, it's who's standing "WITH US" next to the mirror. —FF*

It's a sad life when you don't see anything good in you, but it's even more sad when everyone else sees the same thing. David was used to people doubting him his entire life. He was thrown in the back of the sheep pen. He was not even considered by his own father when Samuel was looking for the next king. He was passed by as usual.

David must have felt the same way I and many other kids did when we were in school. I was that kid that was chosen *last* every time two captains had to pick their teams. I was *that* kid. The last one standing up against the fence, forced to be on a team that nobody wanted me on.

However, when David reached for those stones in the stream, something told him to look beyond his distorted image and to affix his eyes on not what *he* can do but what *God* can do through him.

David walked toward Goliath and his eyes weren't on the giant—his eyes were fixed on God. His eyes weren't on the stones, or the sling, or the defeated lion and bear... or even on himself. His eyes were fixed on God!

You can't win these battles on your own, but God can win them for you. Recognize that these battles are God's and when people are looking down on you, God is cheering FOR YOU!

Tiger Woods: Kicked while he was down, wins the Masters 2019.

How long were you waiting for that fist pump? If you were one of those people who kicked *Tiger* while he was down, perhaps you weren't expecting that vintage fist pump!

I had been waiting ten years for it, and it finally came. Tiger Woods gave me the pump on Sunday, April 14, 2019 by winning his fifth Masters tournament at Augusta National.

Woods' putt at No. 18 finished off a 2-under final round (and a 13-under tournament) in a legendary performance. Woods threw his arms in the air in celebration, a moment that his true fans had been waiting for all day, all weekend, all decade.

Woods was tied for the lead with five holes to go... four holes to go...

There's nothing like seeing Tiger in contention! I had been waiting for that moment since... when? Was it 2008? That's the last time Woods won a major, at the U.S. Open, before his personal life took a turn in 2009 with the fallout from extramarital affairs. He had his entire life exposed. He battled injuries on the long road back to the top. Yet Woods played on. He finished in the top five at Augusta three times this decade, but so many never thought he'd ever win again.

At the young age of twenty-one-years-old, we were introduced to a fist pump and a presence that would revolutionize the sport.

Woods jumped into our living rooms and prompted us to hit a driving range. His impact on golf was unmatched. There was simply nothing like it.

For those who have been watching the last twenty-two years, this is the moment we will always point to. Woods' most dominant moment will always be from 1997, but this will be the most memorable moment of his career. It was every bit as iconic as we thought it would be; right down to the symmetry between his hug with his father Earl then and the one with his son Charlie on Sunday, April 14, 2019.

There is nothing quite like the "Tiger Effect." Go ahead, kick him while he's down, but it doesn't mean he won't get back up.

From 1997-2009 he won 14 major titles. He won the 2008 U.S. Open with a torn ACL. Then from 2009–2017, he suffered a neck injury, sprained MCL, achilles injury, three back surgeries in three years and falls out of top 1,000 in world rank!

So, the next time you feel you are on the ground and nobody is around to pick you up, remember what the word of God says:

Surely the arm of the Lord is not too short to save, nor His ear too dull to hear **(Isaiah 59:1)**.

CHAPTER SIX

DISSED BY MAN—CON.TINUED WITH GOD

"The body of Christ is a lot bigger than I thought."

I grew up in the eighties with music like Duran Duran, The Cure, Depeche Mode, Motley Crue, and Bon Jovi. However, I was more involved in the hip hop and R&B genre: groups like Run D.M.C., Whoodini, Onyx, N.W.A., Ready for the world, and Expose.

I was a break dancer in the 1980s. Instead of fighting we would *"take it to the floor,"* which meant let's compete in dance against each other. Whoever is better is the winner.

At times dancers will still cross the line when dancing against one another. They would do what in the streets is called a *diss*. Which simply in short means dis-respect. A dancer would do an inappropriate dance move that would disrespect and usually would end up in a fight anyway.

In this life, we are going to get dissed by man.

*How can you say to your brother, "Brother, let me take the speck out of your eye," when you yourself **fail** to see the plank in your own eye? You hypocrite, first take the plank out of your eye, and then you will see clearly to remove the speck from your brother's eye* **(Luke 6:42).**

One of the first churches I visited after my discontinuance was **Oasis L.A.** with the phenomenal *Pastors Philip and Holly Wagner.* After that Sunday morning church service, one of the pastors walked over to me and said; ***"The body of Christ is lot bigger than you thought, right?"*** *I responded with my eye balls so big and said – Wow!*

In the days of Noah, the Lord saw how great the wickedness of the human race had become on the earth, and that every inclination of the thoughts of the human heart was only evil all the time. However, there was one man who found favor in the sight of God... NOAH.

1. **God commanded him to make an Ark.**
2. **He instructed him to take his entire family in it with him.**
3. **He also instructed him to take every kind of food in it with him.**
4. **He tells him to take every kind of animal and its mate with him.**

Then, after Noah did all that God asked him to do, Genesis 7:16 says: *Then the Lord shut him in.* For forty days the flood kept coming on the earth, and as the waters increased they lifted the ark high above the earth.

Just because God decides to SHUT YOU IN, it doesn't mean that He SHUTS YOU OUT. When God shuts you in, He's not giving you the cold shoulder. He's usually protecting you from something. In this case, it was a flood that kept coming for 150 days.

Often, the mistake we make is people SHUT DOWN when they are SHUT IN.

Don't listen to critics, just get the job done. There's another world out there!

Can you imagine being 500-years-old and hearing God say, "OK, get up and build a boat.

- I know there isn't any water anywhere near here, but it's going to rain.
- I know you've never seen rain before, but there's going to be a lot of it."

Can you imagine not only agreeing to build a boat at the age of 500, but also continuing to build that boat for 100 years in the midst of mockery and the laughing of others?

1. *What are you building a boat for, really?*
2. *There's no water around here!*
3. *Rain? What's rain?*

4. *You think that thing you are building is going to keep you safe from a bunch of water that's supposed to flood the whole world?*

These types of thoughts we say to ourselves, or words that others may say to us, can tempt us to quit being a Christian altogether because we have this faulty notion in our minds that once we get saved we will suddenly be perfect.

There is an entire world to see outside the ark! The ark could be our place of comfort and at times think that's where God wants us to stay for a lifetime. Think about it. Everything we need is in the ark: family, food, warmth, leadership, safety, covering, reproduction potential. However, as my friend told me that came to visit me from Los Angeles, *Some people just get popped out of a place that they are too big for!* **The body of Christ is a lot bigger than I thought.**

Ever since I was popped out of my ark, I've met so many pastors and brothers and sisters in Christ that are part of the body of Christ. From Elevation Church to the neighborhood church around the corner from me. Don't get me wrong... I had a lot of brothers and sisters where I come from. But, up until now, I'm assuming that we were only family if I remained in their church body. But the body at large is so much bigger outside of just one organization. There are way more church conferences to attend and a lot more preachers to hear than just the same ones year after year for the last thirty-two years. My spirit has been reignited in just one year from attending and meeting so many other pastors and members of the body of Christ. Not the body of a church, but the body of **"THEE"** church. Catholics are my brothers and sisters, Mormons, Muslims, and all other religions are my family. Why is that? Because God created us all the same way. From the dust of the earth in his image. I choose to believe that Muslims can convert over to Christianity just like Nicodemus who was a member of the Jewish ruling council in Jesus' days on earth converted.

Lazarus was SHUT IN a tomb longer than he was supposed to. He was "shut in" for four days. But Jesus said: this sickness will not end in death. Jesus, once more deeply moved, came to the tomb. It was a cave with a stone laid across the entrance. "Take away the stone," He said.

"But, Lord," said Martha, the sister of the dead man, "by this time there is a bad odor, for he has been there four days."

Then Jesus said, "Did I not tell you that if you believe, you will see the glory of God?"

When he had said this, Jesus called in a loud voice, "Lazarus, come out!" **(John 11:38-40,43).**

Lazarus was there *one day too long*. Not even Jesus was in his tomb longer than three days. Some of us have been trapped in your tiny world. What do you think you are doing? There are so many more people to meet outside of your ark. I dare you today to visit God's world! It's way bigger than you think. He created it for us. Go visit another church and see with your own eyes how big God is.

God created a womb on purpose, just like He created a cocoon. There are certain places in life that we are only to stay for an allotted amount of time. Then pop out!

Then He said to the woman, "I will sharpen the pain of your pregnancy, and in pain you will give birth. And you will desire to control your husband, but he will rule over you," (**Genesis 3:16**).

FROM WOUNDED—TO WOMB-DID

Some readers may think that this book focuses too much on hurt, being hurt, or always hurt. The truth of the matter is that we all get hurt but some people can just hide it better or tolerate it better than others. But, we all get hurt. Jesus was hurt and was not ashamed to let it be known. He knew HURT was part of his call and involves the human body period. The scripture say that He was **WOUNDED** for our transgressions. There is always a reason for hurt. We come into this world crying and we leave crying. Jesus did. I don't always agree with the causes of hurt but I agree with the results of it.

> *We come into this world crying and we leave crying. Jesus did. —FF*

Let's move from **WOUNDED** to what the **WOMB-DID**.

Why is it that God perfectly designed a woman to carry her child in the womb for nine months? Because that's when it's estimated that a baby is *fully developed* (forty weeks). Yes, the truth is that it is also possible for a child to be birthed sooner than the nine-month period, however, this is what is called a *premature birth*. God don't desire premature churches, or premature Christians. Therefore, trust that the full development of being in the *womb of God* (your waiting period) is exactly how God tailored it: "Well-developed, not a preemie."

Last year, Franklyn Graham held one of his many crusades in my city. I was honored to be invited to a luncheon with him and his team the afternoon of the evening's mass event. As he began to pour out his heart to the pastors and guests that were in that room, he told the story of his father's death. From the best of my recollection he goes on to say that when his mother Ruth Graham died on June 14, 2007, his father "Billy Graham said that he would live to be 100-years-old." I believe that Rev. Graham was 89-years-old at this time. On February 21, 2018, Billy Graham died. He was 99-years-old.

Franklyn Graham then tells us that the President of the United States called him to express his condolences. He was truly grateful for the call. He then tells the President of the United States the story on how his father said that he would live to be 100-years-old! From the best of my recollection, the president replied, *"Well I guess that your father had that one wrong..."* Franklyn said, *"No, my father didn't get that wrong, you are not counting the nine months he lived in his mother's womb. That would make my father 100-years-old!"*

God created the world and galaxy in six days, not overnight. Every month of development counts in the womb!

CHILD DEVELOPMENT:

At conception, this very moment, the genetic makeup is complete, including the sex of the baby.

...at 4 Weeks

At this the child has formed his face and neck. And the lungs, stomach, and liver start to develop.

...at 8 Weeks

Eyelids and ears are forming, the arms and legs are well-formed.

...at 12 Weeks

The baby starts to make its own movements. You can hear the baby's heartbeat.

...at 16 Weeks

The baby's eyes can blink, and the baby's fingers and toes have fingerprints

...at 20 Weeks

The baby can suck his thumb, yawn, stretch, and make faces.

...at 24 Weeks

The baby now responds to sounds. He hiccups as well.

...at 32 Weeks

The baby's skin has wrinkles as a layer of fat starts to form under the skin.

...at 36 Weeks

The brain has been developing rapidly. Lungs are nearly fully developed.

I guess what I'm trying to say is that every moment counts when you feel hidden and unseen. When everyone else is getting the glory, God is doing your forming.

JOSEPH WAS A PERSON THAT WAS IN GOD'S WOMB.

"Joseph, one of Jacob's twelve sons, was obviously the favorite. Hated by his brothers for this, he was sold to slave traders." "Through Joseph, we learn how suffering, no matter how unfair, develops strong character and deep wisdom in the long run."

"I'm sure Joseph knew that his brothers didn't like him too much, but I'm also sure that he never would have imagined that his brothers would sell him to slave traders, but that's exactly what they did!" Most of us here know the story of this seventeen-year-old teenager. He was spoiled rotten.

His dad's favorite son with a fashioned designer robe of many colors…

In Joseph's day, everyone had a robe or cloak.

Robes were used for..

1. Warmth
2. To bundle up belongings for a trip
3. To wrap babies
4. To sit on
5. To serve as security for a loan

Most robes were..

1. Knee high
2. Short sleeved
3. Very plain

Joseph's robe was…

1. The kind that was only worn by royalty
2. Long sleeved
3. Ankle length
4. Very colorful

Scholars believe that it was this robe that broke the camel's back with Joseph's brothers that caused the turning against him.

Joseph had what I call "Innocent Ignorance."

Joseph had no clue that he was bragging when he animated the two dreams he had. *The "Binding sheaves" and the "Moon and the stars."*

To top it all off, he is telling these dreams to his brothers in that fancy robe of his! His brothers sat and listened to the dreams in their plain and dirty robes after a hard day's work in the fields.

Joseph was overconfident and didn't know it! He had a natural self-assurance that was way bigger than his natural height!

It wasn't all his fault though. Sometimes it could be the parent's fault. In Joseph's case, his father didn't help in keeping him humble.

"Favoritism in families may be unavoidable, but its divisive effects should be minimized. Parents may not be able to change their feelings toward a favorite child, but they can change their actions toward the others."

At the end of the day it was unbearable to his older brothers, who conspired against him. In spite of Joseph and his father's fault, he was molded by pain and survived where most of us would have failed. He would have never been able to "gain" without a "loss." The biggest test of humility for winners is a great loss. I've always admired boxers who lose in the ring and credit the opponent who the

> *The biggest test of humility for winners is a great loss.—FF*

judges deemed fit for the win. The ones who come up with a million reasons as to why they feel they should have won, should have never accepted, or called for the fight in the first place.

Joseph's brothers had what I call "Immature Jealousy."

Could jealousy ever make you feel like killing someone? Before saying *of course not*, look at what happened in this story. Ten MEN were willing to kill their teenage brother over a robe and a few reported dreams.

Someone once said:

"I've seen forty-year-old men act like thirteen-year-old boys, and I've seen thirteen-year-old boys act like men."

Their deep jealousy had grown into an ugly rage, completely blinding them to what was right. The longer you cultivate jealous feelings, the harder it is to uproot them. Just be "you," don't worry about those around you who you think are better than you. It's okay!

There's no grace on your life to be somebody else. It's a whole lot easier to be you. You don't have to pretend, you don't have to perform. Relax! Be you.

Yes! Sometimes just being you is what can cause people to feel jealous. They get jealous because they wish they could be themselves. Joseph was just being him. It's sad to say that the closest people around him would have had him rather be a fake than to be fabulous. People will leave your side but don't worry—new people will show up. Why? Because you are not changing what God has made you YOU. When the leading soft drink company in the world, *Coca-Cola,* started to lose their leading position is when they began to get intimidated with *Pepsi-Cola.* So, they changed their formula and started to cycle downward.

Joseph's brothers were competing with someone who was not in same race they were in. Don't get distracted trying to keep up with someone who is running on another track field. We are all running the same race, just on different running tracks. Stay on your track, stay in your lane.

If Saul understood this, he would have been happy for David, then he wouldn't have missed his destiny. Saul committed suicide because he couldn't handle the happiness of other people. Happy people are so focused on their own goals, they don't have time to look around to see how everybody else is living. Happy people don't get intimidated by others, they get *inspired.*

> *Happy people are so focused on their own goals, they don't have time to look around to see how everybody else is living.—FF*

Joseph may have had an *Innocent Ignorance* and his brother an *Immature Jealousy,* but one thing that was not taken from Joseph was the favor.

Joseph added quiet wisdom to his resume. His confidence in God won the hearts of everyone he came across in his lifetime.

- **Favor—with Potiphar**
- **Favor—with the prison warden**
- **Favor—with the other prisoners**
- **Favor—with the Pharaoh**
- **Favor—with those "ten brothers" of his years down the road**

Joseph had what I call a "Womb-Did" experience with God.

1. He was betrayed and deserted by his family.
   » But God was with him!
2. He was left to starve in a cistern that his brothers threw him into.
   » But God was with him!
3. He was heartbroken when his brothers ripped the robe his dad made for him.
   » But God was with him!
4. He was exposed to sexual temptation.
   » But God was with him!
5. He was punished for doing the right thing. He didn't have sex with that woman but was still punished for it.

» But God was with him!

6. He was accused of rape.

   » But God was with him!

7. He endured long imprisonment and was forgotten by all those he helped.

   » But God was with him!

8. Joseph's biological daddy wasn't with him through it all.

   » But God was with him!

If you read Joseph's response to each and every one of these *Womb-Did* experiences—his response was always a positive one! When Potiphar's wife tried to entice him, his response was, *"How could I do such a wicked thing? It would be a great sin against God."*

"For years, experts said that no one would ever be able to run a mile in under four minutes. They studied the human body and thought it would collapse under that much pressure. Scientists said it was not only dangerous to try, but it was literally impossible. But a young man named 'Roger Bannister' didn't believe the negative reports. He didn't let his mind become conditioned to thinking it could not be done. In May 1954, he made history by running a mile in under four minutes. What's interesting is that forty-six days later, someone else broke the four-minute mile. Within ten years, 336 people had run the mile in under four minutes."

This kind response is what took him from the *pit*, to the *palace,* sitting right next to the *pharaoh.* Joseph's pit was just a pit stop.

Joseph learned a lesson in the womb he couldn't have learned if he was born a "preemie." After all those years of hell to heaven, a family reunion finally happened when Joseph's brothers showed up in need

> *Joseph's pit was just a pit stop. —FF*

and didn't realize that it was their younger brother that they were begging from. He went from slave to ruler.

SLAVE: Joseph's brothers would have never imagined their spoiled brother to survive as a slave.

Joseph faced a thirty-day journey through the dessert, probably chained hand and foot. He would be treated like baggage and once in Egypt would be sold as a piece of merchandise. He was no longer a "person," he was a "puppet."

RULER: Joseph was now second in command to the king of Egypt!

Then Pharaoh said to his officials, "Isn't this the man we need? Are we going to find anyone else who has God's spirit in him like this?" So, Pharaoh said to Joseph, "You're the man for us. God has given you the inside story—no one is as qualified as you in experience and wisdom. From now on, you're in charge of my affairs; all my people will report to you. Only as king will I be over you." So, Pharaoh commissioned Joseph: "I'm putting you in charge of the entire country of Egypt." Then Pharaoh removed his signet ring from his finger and slipped it on Joseph's hand. He outfitted

*him in robes of the best linen and put a gold chain around his
neck. He put the second-in-command chariot at his disposal, and
as he rode people shouted "Bravo!" Joseph was in charge of the
entire country of Egypt. Pharaoh told Joseph, "I am Pharaoh, but
no one in Egypt will make a single move without your stamp of
approval,"* **(Genesis 41:38-44).**

*Joseph couldn't hold himself in any longer, keeping up
a front before all his attendants. He cried out, "Leave! Clear
out—everyone leave!" So, there was no one with Joseph when he
identified himself to his brothers. But his sobbing was so violent
that the Egyptians couldn't help but hear him. The news was soon
reported to Pharaoh's palace.*

*Joseph spoke to his brothers: "I am Joseph. Is my father really
still alive?" But his brothers couldn't say a word. They were
speechless—they couldn't believe what they were hearing and
seeing.*

*"Come closer to me," Joseph said to his brothers. They came
closer. "I am Joseph, your brother whom you sold into Egypt. But
don't feel badly, don't blame yourselves for selling me. God was
behind it. God sent me here ahead of you to save lives. There has
been a famine in the land now for two years; the famine will
continue for five more years—neither plowing nor harvesting.
God sent me on ahead to pave the way and make sure there was
a remnant in the land, to save your lives in an amazing act of
deliverance. So, you see,* **it wasn't you who sent me here but God,"**
(Genesis 45:1-8).

It wasn't the enemy or your enemy that kept you hidden in the pit, it was God who sent you there.

Some people just "HATE" dreamers:

Dr. King once said; *"You can kill the dreamer, but you can't kill the dream."* He also said: *"We must learn to live together as brothers or perish together as fools."* Joseph's brothers sure enough nearly perish together as fools.

Dreamers always shake up a world, and you're never too old to dream!

1. **Vera Wang**—The fashion designer Vera Wang was forty-years-old when she opened her flagship bridal salon at the (Karla) Carlyle Hotel in New York.

2. **Henry Ford**—The founder of "Ford" automobile was forty-five-years-old when his Model T car was introduced to the public in 1908.

3. **Reed Hastings**—The CEO of Netflix was forty-seven-years-old when he finally got his first streaming.

> *Dreamers always shake up a world, and you're never too old to dream!*
> *—FF*

The founders of McDonald's, Coca Cola, and Kentucky Fried Chicken—Were all over the age fifty when they established their businesses.

You are never too old or too young to dream! Martin Luther King Jr. was twenty-five-years-old when he started dreaming and Joseph was just seventeen-years-old when he started dreaming.

The other day I asked my eight-year-old daughter Hannah, *What do you want to be when you grow up?* She answered immediately, *My first career I want to be a doctor, my second career I want to be a lawyer, and for my third career I want to work for the police department.*

Dreams that happen at 2:00a.m. are overnight dreams, dreams that happen through pits, valleys, and break-ups are the ones that become a reality.

It all begins with a dream. I suppose *Walt Disney* was right when he said, *"It's a small world after all."* and *"This all began with a mouse."*

Get out there and meet the rest of your Christian family!

Whenever you feel you've been dissed, remember: "What, then, shall we say in response to these things? If God is for us, who can be against us?? (ROMANS 8:31).

> *Dreams that happen at 2:00a.m. are overnight dreams, dreams that happen through pits, valleys, and break-ups are the ones that become a reality. —FF*

CHAPTER SEVEN

THAT'S THE GUY WHO STOLE MY BIKE!

"Hey, that's mine."

There's a true story of a young black man in the ghettos. He was fortunate in that he had both of his parents, and they struggled to make ends meet. But for his birthday that year they had scraped together enough money to pay for a brand new bicycle. A few days later someone stole it. Enraged, the boy went looking for the thief and in the process of his search he encountered a policeman. The policeman asked him what he was going to do if he caught the boy who stole it and the boy said that he didn't know.

It was obvious to the cop that if this boy ever did find the person who stole his bike, he might not only lose the bike but be beaten terribly in any fight that ensued, so he asked the boy if he would like to go the gym with him. The boy agreed, and they went together to a nearby sports center where the policeman began teaching the boy how to box.

That boy was named Cassius Clay. Later he changed his name to Mohammed Ali and became one of the greatest fighters to ever enter the ring. But while Mohammed Ali was similar to many of the fighters of that time—he worked out just like they did, he boxed and sparred, and ran for miles in preparation for every fight—he had one distinguishing difference that gave him the edge whenever he put on his gloves.

Ali said, *"To this day I never found my bike, but every time I got in the ring, I'd look across at my opponent and say to myself, that's the guy who stole my bike!"*

Where's the joy you once had? The laughter, peace, fun, and smile that you possessed in the past? It's been stolen! You didn't give it away; the Devil took it away. It don't belong to him. It's yours! Why does he have it? What you need to do is walk into the enemy's camp and take back what the enemy stole.

Where's the joy you once had? The laughter, peace, fun, and smile that you possessed in the past? It's been stolen! —FF

"That's the guy who stole my family."

"That's the guy who stole my freedom."

"That's the guy who stole my health."

"That's the guy who stole my joy."

"That's the guy who stole my business."

"That's the guy who stole my calling."

When we can always remember what our opponent has done to us in the past, and the desire he has to destroy our future, we will always have a reason to stay mad at the Devil! That's the guy who stole my BIKE!

I remember, about six months into my *discontinuance*, a friend of mine drove from Los Angles to visit me. I gave him the short version of what had happened to me and our church. I mentioned to him, *"I guess some people get launched out, and others get kicked out."* He then looked at me with a big smile on his face and said, *"And others get popped out."*

The interpretation of what he was telling me is that people can get too big—sooner or later they MUST COME OUT.

This is what happened to Jesus when they tried to bury Him. Jesus was too big to remain in a borrowed tomb. I believe this is why His tomb was borrowed. He wasn't going to need it but for just three days!

Normally, the ordinary criminal would die four to six days after he was placed on a cross.

But this wasn't the case for Jesus. His maltreatment and torture was so intense that He died approximately six hours later from the time He was raised on the cross.

> *Jesus was too big to remain in a borrowed tomb. I believe this is why His tomb was borrowed. He wasn't going to need it but for just three days!* —FF

After His gruesome "beat down" from His cross walk on the Villa de La Rosa, and after He took His final breath on that center cross, He then would be:

1. **Pulled down**
2. **Let down**
3. **Put down**
4. **Looked down**

Before God can use a man, He cuts him deep. Jesus was cut deep before He was raised up.

We're talking about the king of kings. After he was *pulled down, let down, put down* he eventually was being *looked down* upon by all who were in attendance while his cross laid flat on the ground. Although he was "pulled down," "let down," "put down," "looked down," he wasn't "kept down."

> *Before God can use a man, He cuts him deep. Jesus was cut deep before He was raised up. —FF*

> *Although he was "pulled down," "let down," "put down," "looked down," he wasn't "kept down." —FF*

Doubters, death, and *devils* couldn't keep him down.

The government plastered a stone that weighed anywhere between 2,000 to 4,000 pounds, 6 feet in diameter, and 1 foot thick. They rolled it in front of the tomb. Placed guards to watch it 24/7.

From the very beginning with Lucifer's fall from heaven, he's wanted to have supremacy over God. From the fall of man, in the beginning with Adam & Eve, the Devil celebrated joy when there was a separation between God and man. When Jesus was born, the devil tried to kill Him using king Herod to kill all male children. At the temptation of Jesus, the Devil tried to get Him to take a shortcut that would have defeated why God the Father sent him. And as I wrote in chapter four, at the Garden of Gethsemane, when Jesus was sweating and thinking of changing His mind to go to the cross, Satan tried again.

I truly believe that the Devil and all his legions recorded the victory in hell when Jesus died on the cross. I'm sure the news was, *It is done, Jesus is over, Jesus went down, we can now take control of the world.*

But the Bible says that Satan and his demons got a personal visit by Jesus Himself. He descended into the Devil's camp for three days to preach to the captives. He took back the keys of eternal death. I could picture Jesus speaking through the corridors of hell, *That's the guy who stole my bike!*

Then, for the next forty days, Jesus appeared to the disciples at various times and places with the bike in His hand (emphasis added). It was simply a physical impossibility for Jesus to be at so many different places in one day. These appearances therefore revealed that His glorified body didn't have the same limitations His earthly body possessed before His resurrection.

The Bible makes it clear that in His glorified condition He was able to appear, disappear, and travel great distances. Given the fact that He was to supernaturally pass through a wall, or the locked door of a house, where He proved doubting Thomas wrong when He showed him His marked hand and side.

Jesus went from a locked tomb, through a brick wall, and vanished into an empty sky with a *bike in His hand* (emphasis added).

Going back to the Garden of Gethsemane in chapter four of this book. When Jesus was pleading with His father to take from Him *the cup of horror.*

After falling to His knees three times to ask if it could be removed, He finally *stands up* for good.

Don't let life's *discontinuances* stand taller than you! Jesus stood up for one reason: to move on and to get going forward!

1. **Adam failed in the garden.**
2. **The second Adam (Jesus) stood up in the garden.**

In the beginning of *Fernando Vargas'* career of professional boxing, the crowds showed up because of the opponents he would **lay flat** on their face. Towards the end of his career, crowds showed up because *Fernando Vargas* **refused to stay flat** on his face. If you study the times Vargas lost by way of knockout, he was NEVER counted out ten seconds laid on the floor of the canvas by a referee. He always got back up again before the referee counted to ten. I mean always! At times, he didn't even know if he had won or lost the fight because that's how disoriented he was. He always had the heart of an Aztec warrior in that ring.

You and I ought to have the heart of The Lord of the warrior! Because the Lord *is* a warrior, and that's His name.

> *Someone that knows his DESTINY of tomorrow, works with DETERMINATION today. —FF*

Someone that knows his DESTINY of tomorrow, works with DETERMINATION today.

In boxing, when a champion is defending his title, the amount of rounds the bout is scheduled for is twelve. Non-champions fight just ten rounds; if you are a champion, the additional two are what is called the "championship rounds."

Sometimes, I know it feels like you can't fight anymore, but remember, you are a champion! Fight! Fight! Fight!

Unless the messenger is the message, his preaching is just a poem.

This is why later in life after Jesus ascended into heaven, His disciples were able to die a gruesome death just like Him, because Jesus walked His sermons, not preached them.

It's easy to wear a cross, but harder to bear the cross. It's clear that the blessing always comes after the beating.

My spiritual son *Jonathon* recently passed of leukemia. He

> *It's easy to wear a cross, but harder to bear the cross. —FF*

was a fighter till his very last breath. My wife and I rushed to the emergency room the day he was diagnosed, and three years later we rushed to *City of Hope* where he breathed his last breath. I couldn't believe the fight in him. His lungs were slowly filling with liquid. The doctors did not want to operate on him because of the risks of death on the operating table. *Jonathon* chose to wait patiently, fighting as his lungs filled one hour at a time. I believe he did this for two reasons:

He was a fighter that had faith God would heal him.

If God decided to take him, he wanted as many people to see him alive one last time.

I couldn't believe my eyes when his mother and I gently nudged him back down to his bed a total of three times as he tried to get up and walk out that hospital within five minutes. His lungs were filled with ninety-nine percent of liquid and he could no longer breath. But the fight in him said—*Get up!* The third and final time he attempted to get up and walk out, we again gently nudged him again back on his bed. Approximately sixty seconds later he inhaled his last breath and passed from this life to eternal life. One of the last texts he sent me, his signature read *"sincerely, one of Fernie's guys."*

Jonathon also went to heaven with a bike in his hand. I miss him so much. This was the poem wrote for his eulogy.

"I remember your face that Sunday afternoon
It was bright as the sun-no sign of gloom
"I have leukemia cancer," you said: as a matter of fact.

You had so much faith, you stayed intact.
You were upset not cause of cancer's nerve
You were upset cause you weren't able to serve.
You had a responsibility at church that week
From your hospital bed, you still took a peek.
Thank God for facetime, you were still in church
From week to week you would search and search.
What's happening in service today?
I don't want to miss out on what God has to say?
Your attitude is what carried you "Jon",
Without it you wouldn't have made it this long.
The cancer attacked you that vicious disease.
But all it did was keep you on your knees.
But still through it all you held that smile
You kept it on your face till that very last mile.
I'm going to miss you at my house all those days and nights
Now I need a new example of someone who fights.
You did what you could do, the best you can
Last Tuesday you saw, the great I am.
So-go on my friend, my spiritual son
I'm sure when you saw Jesus, all you could do was run.
Into his arms and hugged him tight
He hugged you back and said no more fight.
He said; You can rest up here and enjoy this view
Your entire family will be right behind you.
You showed your family how to get up here
Keep applauding them Jonno we can hear your cheer!

Now, I just wish you had a phone up in heaven
I tried emailing you–the Gmail that ends with seven?
You always did what Pastor Fernie said
Not this time Jonno, you've been led.
Led to the place were all trying to be
Wait for us Jon, in eternity"

So, what are you waiting for? **Go get your bike back. As you go get it, tell the devil; "Hey, that's mine!"**

CHAPTER EIGHT

STARS WITH SCARS

"Stars weren't born one, they became one."

The motion picture *A Star is Born* with actors/artists Bradley Cooper and Lady Gaga was a "star" in itself, receiving twenty-four major nominations in 2019 and winning three awards at the 2019 academy awards.

Most aspiring artists love the heights that Lady Gaga achieved in the movie, but often ignore the costs to get there! The film starts with popular singer Jackson Maine (Bradley Cooper) getting ready to perform to a sold-out audience, but only after secretly taking a few pills. He sings the song "Black Eyes," which the crowd loves. Meanwhile, Ally (Lady Gaga) is a songwriter working at a catering hall. She is seen apparently breaking up with someone over the phone before joining her friend Ramon (Anthony Ramos) at work where she gets constantly chewed out by her boss Bryan (Jacob Schick). After work, Ally heads toward a performance while singing to herself. *Stars weren't born one, they became one.*

When it was evening on that day, the first day of the week, and the doors of the house where the disciples

had met were locked for fear of the Jews, Jesus came and stood among them and said, "Peace be with you." After He said this, He showed them His hands and His side. Then the disciples rejoiced when they saw the Lord. Jesus said to them again, "Peace be with you. As the Father has sent me, so I send you." When He had said this, He breathed on them and said to them, "Receive the Holy Spirit. If you forgive the sins of any, they are forgiven them; if you retain the sins of any, they are retained."

*But Thomas (called Didymus, or "Twin"), one of the twelve, was not with them when Jesus came. So, the other disciples told him, "We have seen the Lord." But he said to them, **"Unless I see the mark of the nails in his hands, and put my finger in the mark of the nails and my hand in his side, I will not believe,"*** **(John 20:19-25).**

A former army soldier revealed that when he went into the Army, he was given a physical medical examination. He was asked if he had any scars or identifying marks. He answered, *"No."*

The medic at the table said, *"Boy, everybody has some scars. You better tell me yours or I'll have to take you outside and give you some of your own!"*

All of us in ministry have scars. Every successful businessman, artist, or anyone that has influence have scars. You can't be successful in life without them.

Everyone wants to be a **"David"** but nobody wants to be one of *"David's Mighty Men."*

Many people want the pulpit but refuse to work the parking.

In the Bible, Thomas **demands** to see the scars upon the hands of Jesus. Before someone follows a leader, they want to know where the leader has walked! Success is NOT given, it's worked for. Today's generation don't want to follow an inheritance, they want to follow an authentic.

> *Every successful businessman, artist, or anyone that has influence have scars. You can't be successful in life without them.* —FF

Thomas was full of doubt and when he is told by one of the other disciples, *"We have seen the Lord."* Thomas responds with some honest and sincere doubt. He has a **"gotta see it to believe it"** attitude. Today is no different. People got to see it to believe it! The millennials are tired of being told what to do, that want to see what you can do.

> *The millennials are tired of being told what to do, that want to see what you can do.* —FF

Thomas looks at the other disciples and says, *"Unless I see the mark of the nails in his hands and put my finger in the mark of the nails and my hand in his side, I will not believe."*

This is a perfect example what can happen if you just miss one church service. *Thomas was missing the day that Jesus supernaturally walked through the walls to show Himself. What a church service that must have been!*

Everyone wants to be stars, but can they show me some scars? If I were to look at your hands, will I see nail marks? If I were to look at your feet, will I see blisters? Do you have any scars to PROVE who you say you are?

> *Everyone wants to be stars, but can they show me some scars? —FF*

Every "Star" has a "Scar." I know some people look at a person that has scars on their body and see it as sickening. For me, scars are so attractive. They are attractive to followers.

JOHN WALSH

John Walsh born in Auburn, New York, is known for the TV show *America's Most Wanted.* What most people don't know is that he is a man with a broken heart and full of scars.

On July 27, 1981, John's wife, Revé, let their six-year-old son watch a small group of older boys play video games at a Sears store in Hollywood, Florida, while she walked a few aisles away to shop for a lamp. When she returned to the video game section, she was frightened to find that their son was gone. She was only gone for about seven minutes.

Police records indicate that a seventeen-year-old security guard asked four boys to leave the department store and that Adam was believed to be one of them. She then told a Sears associate, who announced over the intercom for her son to meet his mother at one of the information desks. Reve (mother) later said that she had no confidence that her son would be able to locate the desks. Her son Adam was never reunited again with her or JOHN (the father). It is suspected that Adam was abducted near the front exterior of the store.

Sixteen days after the abduction, his severed head was found in a drainage canal more than 120 miles away from home. His other remains were never recovered.

This little boy's name was "Adam Walsh," son of John Walsh. Today, we know John Walsh as host of *America's Most Wanted* and the show on CNN—*The Hunt*.

A VISION IS USUALLY BIRTHED OUT OF PAIN.

It was after the pain of his abducted and murdered son that he began to do something about the kidnapping problem in AMERICA.

Ever since that crisis, John Walsh has been the spearhead for many organizations and events.

By the late 1980s, many malls, department stores, supermarkets, and other such retailers have adopted what is known as a *Code Adam*, a movement first introduced by Wal-Mart stores in the southeastern United States. A *Code Adam* is announced when a child is missing in a store or if a child is found by a store employee. If the child is lost or missing, all doors are to be locked and a store employee is posted at every exit, while a description of the child is generally broadcast over the intercom system.

Everyone wants to be "STARS" with no "SCARS." Everyone wants to be called one of Christ's disciples but don't want to die the death of one.

Again, Jesus said, "Peace be with you! As the Father has sent me, so I send you", (**John 20:21**).

Scars are nothing to be afraid about. Think about it; these are the first words that Jesus said when seeing the disciples for the first time after His murder... *"As the Father has sent me, so I send you."*

> *Everyone wants to be called one of Christ's disciples but don't want to die the death of one. —FF*

What he was saying was: *If I get murdered so do you! If I get scars so will you!* Stars know that the blessings come with beatings.

Jesus was not famous; He was a star. Not the star that most people want to be. Most people want to be that star that has an enormous bank account, over one million followers, and stopped everywhere his feet tread. NO! Jesus was a different kind of star. Jesus is our hero, not our celebrity. He is *the bright and morning star*. The star that would bring light because of the price He endured for our darkness.

> *Stars know that the blessings come with beatings. —FF*

> *Jesus is our hero, not our celebrity. —FF*

What do these scars mean?

For Thomas, it serves as proof of the resurrection. Every successful person will have doubters. The only thing that will shut doubters up are S.C.A.R.S!

Some people only throw rocks at the parade they think they're supposed to be in. When people talk behind your back, they are behind you for a reason.

John Maxwell says:

- When hiding from our DOUBTERS—We lose momentum in life.
- When hindering our DOUBTERS—We lose focus in life.
- When hurting our DOUBTERS—We lose integrity of life.

Jesus didn't do any of this to doubting Thomas; he simply just displayed HIS SCARS. These scars became part of the fabric of evidence that the resurrection was not a rumor or a figment of imagination. The resurrection was real. Scars prove to people that you've been there and are still doing that.

There is something about scars that seems to make a person "more human."

> *Scars prove to people that you've been there and are still doing that. —FF*

"I learned my right from left because of the nail scar on my right foot."

"I learned to never jump backwards on my bed because of the scar on the back of my skull."

"I learned to hold a knife the right way because of the scar on my left finger."

"I learned not to break bottles against a pole because of the scar on the palm of my right hand."

"I learned not to stick my face in front of a German shepherd because of the scar on my forehead."

We are sometimes suspicious about people who seem to be "too perfect": about children who don't seem to have scraped knees, about teenagers who don't show any signs of acne, about models whose hair is perfect and who weigh ninety-five pounds. There is something about our scars that makes us real, believable, and trustworthy to people who want AUTHENTICITY.

The Mongolian General

The Mongolian General addressed his commanders; he stood up and ordered them to tell their troops, "When engaging the enemy look for the Warriors who have scars, avoid them all cost, go after the ones with no scars because the ones who have scars that are still fighting know how to fight and have survived."

Paul the Apostle had scars that he talked about:

*Therefore, in order to keep me from becoming conceited, I was **given** a thorn in my flesh, a messenger of **Satan**, to torment me. Three times I pleaded with the Lord to take it away from me. But He said to me, "My grace is sufficient for you, for my power is made perfect in weakness." Therefore, I will boast all the more gladly about my weaknesses, so that Christ's power may rest on me* **(II Corinthians 12:7-9).**

God never wastes a hurt. What you need to understand is that although you may wish pain had never happened and you may wish circumstances of your life were different, God has allowed you to go through them so that HE could show up in your life.

So many people go through life mad at God and hurt that God allowed them to experience pain. But God's desire is that we take the pain in our lives and we learn to grow from it and be those *stars with scars.*

> *Scars are not a sign of weakness; they are signs of survival, signs of strength. —FF*

How does the process of oil work?

First—The olive is picked.

Second—The olive is cleaned.

Third—The olive is put into a press.

Fourth—The large wheel rolls across it to get the olive oil out.

Fifth—The pure olive oil is separated from the rest.

The anointing is NOT given; it is processed by the behavior of a person. This is why the scripture says: *"Come out from among them, and be ye separate..."* (**2 Corinthians 6:17**).

Scars are not a sign of weakness; they are signs of survival, signs of strength.

Scars shape you in one of three ways:

- Your scars can paralyze you.
- Your scars can make you bitter.
- Your scars can strengthen your character.

I would like to end this chapter by issuing men and women with new names. From here on out, the men's names shall be called **Scarface** and the ladies, **Scarlet.**

CHAPTER NINE

DON'T JUST STAND THERE

"Do something!"

Jesus had just finished spending forty days face-to-face with the apostles after his resurrection. He had given them many different convincing proofs that it was Him, *alive and back from the dead.* He talked with them around the dinner table on many different occasions over these forty days. They talked about the Kingdom of God, the restoration of Israel, and had other personal one-on-one-conversations.

You can sense the urgency from Jesus as he knew that he only had forty days left with them to get in as much as he can "in the flesh" with his men.

It reminds me of when my father passed. Although my father had abandoned me during my teenage years, we did have a reunion later on in my adulthood. Our relationship was the most precious one you can imagine between a sixty-eight-year-old man and a forty-six-year-old son. I could remember the urgency he had to inform me of as much of family history he can before his time came to die.

Jesus must have had a greater urgency when he told the disciples in a conversation, *"Do not leave Jerusalem, but wait for the gift my Father promised... but you will receive power when the Holy Spirit comes on you, and you will be my witnesses in Jerusalem, and in all Judea and Samaria and to the utter most parts of the world,"* **(ACTS 1:8)**.

THE LAST WORDS OF CHRIST ON EARTH:

These were his last words. As they watched, he was taken up and disappeared in a cloud. They stood there, staring into the empty sky. Suddenly two men appeared—in white robes! They said, "You Galileans!—why do you just stand here looking up at an empty sky? **(ACTS 1:9-11)**. It was almost as if the angles were saying:

"DON'T JUST STAND THERE... DO SOMETHING!"

I remember the very first job I had was selling candy door to door for Junior Careers. My second job was sanding cars for my uncle's painting business. My third job was working at a fast food restaurant. My fourth job was working in the roofing business.

While working in roofing, it was very laborious and I would get tired easily. I could remember I would often just climb up the ladder... down the ladder... up the ladder... down the ladder holding an empty bucket in my hand *"Appearing as if I were doing something."*

My prayer is that as you're coming to the end of this book, don't just appear as if the reading alone is going to change your life. **"DO SOMETHING."** Just as it was that day in the disciples' lives in the book of Acts, we have too many Christians just *"standing there staring into an empty sky."* Don't just stand there, do something!

HOW SOON WERE THE APOSTLES SUPPOSED TO DO SOMETHING? Suddenly

"Suddenly two men appeared—in white robes! They said, "You Galileans!—why do you just stand here looking up at an empty sky?" **(ACTS 1:10).**

When I think of the word suddenly the word accelerate comes to mind. When I was growing up in my neighborhood, gang members represented their gangs by something they called **"Throwing up signs." <u>Do you know that God speaks "Sign Language too?"</u>** I'm not saying God is a gang member, but he speaks sign language. The Bible calls it "Signs of the end times."

Jesus said *"I tell you the truth, this generation will certainly not pass away until all "THESE (SIGNS) THINGS" have happened,"* **(MATTHEW 24:34).**

GOD'S SIGN LANGUAGE IS:

1. **Countless people will claim to be the Christ.**
   Since the year 1900, it's been recorded that over 1,100 people have claimed to be the Christ.

2. **The many wars and rumors of wars.**
   No period has witnessed the escalation of wars as has the 20th century.
   The Red Cross has estimated that over 100 million people have been killed in wars since the 20th century.

3. **Pestilences (Plague of a literal disease).**
   Aids – Over 25 million people worldwide are sick with aids and over 100 million infected with (HIV). Not including the so many other diseases.
   Cancer – Virtually over 100 different kinds of cancer now kill over 5 million people every year.

4. **Earthquakes in various places.**
   In 1964 the state of Alaska here in the U.S. was devastated by a massive earthquake measuring 8.4 on the Richter Scale. In the 30 years after that quake, there would follow as many major earthquakes as in the entire previous 2,000 years of world history! Between 1950 and 1991, the major earthquakes around the world tripled in escalation from the first half century. Since 1991 there has been over 35,000 earthquakes that have happened around the world!

Do your own research; approximately 347 earthquakes are reported every seven days.

As I write this book, yesterday, according to the *Science of a Changing World* website at 10:00 a.m., 43 earthquakes were happening at the same time around the world.

5. **Today's age of transportation.**

   "... and many shall run to and fro," (**Daniel 12:4**).

   The phrase *many shall run to and fro* is a clear reference to the ability of mankind to travel to any spot on the globe in a relatively short time. From walking in sandals, riding on donkeys, jets and trips to the moon and mars is how this scripture is being lived out.

6. **Today's age of knowledge.**

   "... and knowledge shall increase" (**Daniel 12:4**).

We've "accelerated" from..

1. The telegraph
2. To the telephone
3. From the telephone to the radio
4. From the radio to the television
5. From the television to computers
6. From computers to the internet
7. From the internet to satellites

Today we can *know* virtually anything in a matter of seconds with a flick of our fingers if we have a modem, smart phone, a computer and an internet service provider.

Many of you downloaded this book in just under sixty seconds when in the past you would have to drive to a bookstore or wait two weeks for a delivery through mail.

I.   THE APOSTLES WERE TO *DO SOMETHING* SUDDENLY!

"Suddenly two men appeared—in white robes! They said, "You Galileans!—why do you just stand here looking up at an empty sky? (ACTS 1:10).* The angels said: "Why do you just stand there?"

When people are at their lowest moments in life, they don't need people to "STAND" with them, they need people to "WORK" with them. There are so many others who have been where you are at and know the pain, danger, and loneliness. Find them! They want to work with you.

It's not how heavy the load is, it's how you carry that load. Just ask the "four men" who carried the paralytic to Jesus and lowered him down that roof. Before there were FIVE GUYS, there was FOUR GUYS.

Just one person would have never been able to carry that paralyzed man to that house, dig through the roof, and lower him down to Jesus. The four friends couldn't wait till after Jesus left that house. They knew that if they were going to have a chance, they would have to make a move now, suddenly, and not tomorrow.

This book is almost over. You need to do something NOW. Not tomorrow, not the next book, NOW!

II. THE APOSTLES WERE TO *LEAVE SOMETHING* SUDDENLY!

So they left the mountain called Olives and returned to Jerusalem. It was a little over half a mile. They went to the upper room they had been using as a meeting place (ACTS 1:12,13). In this case, what the apostle's left was the mountain. They went back to where they were supposed to be (Jerusalem).

On the Mountain that the apostles had to leave behind was a number of experiences….

1. **They were staying with the resurrected Christ.**
    » They saw the nail marks in his hands.
    » They saw the scar on his side.
    » They saw the marks on his brow from the shoved-in crown.
    » They were hanging out with Jesus, something not everybody has the honor to say.
2. **They were getting information from Jesus that no one else was getting.**

When they were together for the last time they asked, "Master, are you going to restore the kingdom to Israel now? Is this the time?"(**Acts 1:6**).

3. **They were having a little bit too much fun!**

   There's a story about an elderly man who was on his death bed ready to die. He called over his wife to his side and said, "Honey, when I die, I want to be cremated." She said, "Why do you want be cremated and NOT PLACED IN A COFFIN?" He answered, "Honey, my entire life of ninety-two years I've been restricted inside a BOX. I don't want to be buried in one."

In another text (Remember when the disciples were up on that mountain at the Transfiguration?) *Jesus took Peter, James, and John and led them up a high mountain* (**Mark 9:2**).

The honest truth is, you may have to leave certain people that are around you that are part of the problem. If a person is constantly feeding you with unhealthy information, it's probably best that you put your relationship on hold for now. **"When a person is so full of themselves, they won't have room for anybody else."**

THE DAZZLING STUFF

There he was transfigured before them. His clothes became dazzling white, whiter than anyone in the world could bleach them **(Mark 9:2-3)**. In today's churches, it's easy enjoying the dazzling stuff.

LED Lighting.
Concert platform.
State of the art digital sound system.
High definition cameras and screens.
LED walls
Worship bands at high and respected levels.

On that mountain, *Elijah* appeared, *Moses* appeared, and they were having a conversation with Jesus on that mountain—"A pretty dazzling sight!" After being with Jesus up on that high mountain, the men who were present with Jesus responded to Him by saying..."Teacher.. this is wonderful," **(Mark 9:5)**. I don't blame them. What a moment they must have been experiencing. Nobody else in this world has ever since experienced a moment such as this.

The time came and your time has arrived in this last chapter of dis.con.tinued. The dazzle of the book will end.

At the opening of this chapter, the time came when Jesus "disappeared" from their sight and the apostles were instructed to go back to Jerusalem and get ready to **DO SOMETHING!**

I know you may not want to end the book, perhaps it's been good therapy, good help and your "go to" every night.

You find yourself saying the same exact words of what the disciples were saying: **This has been wonderful.**

But I'm sorry to be the one to have to tell you, you got to get off your seat, you got to go back! You can't stay here much longer and I'll tell you why!

1. We must accelerate our life and catch up where we stopped living.
2. We don't need a group of **shouting** readers, we need a group full of **serving** readers.
3. Shouting tumbles down walls, serving builds them up!
4. Clap offerings are good at the end of chapters, but sooner or later your hands will stop clapping because of blisters.

The time came when Jesus departed from them in the flesh, but waiting down below in Jerusalem was the promise of His Holy Spirit! When you place this book down, there is going to be a whole lot of disappearing. But the Holy Spirit will never disappear.

III. THE APOSTLES WERE *TO BE* SOMETHING SUDDENLY!

We all must be conscious of the time we have left here on earth. According to what is known as the "Death World

Clock" which is a clock that has a clicking counter with a live number of people being recorded dying by the minute around the world.

106 people die every minute, 6,392 people die every hour. If it's taken you one hour to read this chapter, this is how many people have died since you've been reading chapter nine. You need to accelerate your life. We don' have too much time left.

> *106 people die every minute, 6,392 people die every hour.*

Jesus is ready to rapture his church and some of our good friends may just be left behind. Until we believe that HELL is a real place, we will just be standing in our churches looking up to an empty sky!— DON'T JUST STAND THERE, DO SOMETHING!

> *Until we believe that HELL is a real place, we will just be standing in our churches looking up to an empty sky! —FF*

Think of what you were when you were called. Not many of you were wise by human standards; not many were influential; not many were of noble birth. But God chose the foolish things of the world to shame the wise; God chose the weak things of the world to shame the strong (1 **CORINTHIANS 1:26-27**).

If you were ever told you would amount to anything…

If you were ever told that you were weak and no good for nothing…

If you were ever told that you were unskilled and not even close to qualified…

Then you must be the perfect candidate IN what GOD IS LOOKING FOR.

"*God's criteria is different from the world's criteria.*" We must thank God that He has something different to say about unqualified and dis.con.tinued people.

> *We must thank God that He has something different to say about unqualified and dis.con.tinued people. —FF*

"*For my thoughts are not your thoughts, neither are your ways my ways,*" declares the Lord (**ISAIAH 55:8**).

WHEN IT WAS TIME FOR JESUS TO CHOOSE THE DISCIPLES…

He didn't go to the theological and Bible institutes or seminaries of his day.

So if you ever thought that you weren't good enough for God to use you, I wrote this book to tell you today, It's time for you to renew your thinking. What the world calls devalued, God calls his treasure! What the world calls junk, God calls "Riches stored in secret places."

God has always been looking for people that no one else wants! Before you picked up this book and started reading, you may have been feeling that your life was only good for a junk yard!

I like the way *Eugene Peterson* Message translates 1 Corinthians 1:26, 27: *"Isn't it obvious that God deliberately chose men and women that the culture overlooks and exploits and abuses, chose these 'nobodies' to expose the hollow pretensions of the 'somebodies?'"*

I'm not supposed to be writing this book. I'm not supposed to be one block further than the train tracks of the neighborhood where I grew up. I was not supposed to ever travel to nearly every continent preaching the gospel.

Today, I'm a Bible School graduate with university certifications and a pastor to a courageous church. I know how to order food at a nice restaurant because of Jesus. I can sit with attorneys, celebrities, and millionaires because of Jesus!

I was supposed to die a teenage drug addict! I was supposed to continue living in that beat-down house with no plumbing. I was supposed to raise my kids in that same living room roof that caved in because of a rainy night.

But God chose a man that the culture overlooked and abused, a man that was called a nobody and turned him into a somebody.

When they saw the courage of Peter and John and realized that they were unschooled, ordinary men, they

> *But God chose a man that the culture overlooked and abused, a man that was called a nobody and turned him into a somebody. —FF*

were astonished and they took note that these men had been with Jesus (**ACTS 4:13**).

Your destiny is too great to let people stop you from accelerating. Don't just stand, DO SOMETHING.

There was this country grandfather who took his grandson to town on a donkey. He started off letting his grandson ride the donkey as he walked alongside. Somebody passed by and said, "Look at that selfish little boy making that old man walk."

The grandfather heard it and took the boy off. Then he rode the donkey as his grandson walked by his side. Somebody passed by and said, "Look at that man making that little boy walk while he rides. Hearing that, the grandfather pulled the little boy up with him, and they both started riding the donkey. In a few minutes, another person said, "How cruel of you and the boy to place such a heavy load on that poor donkey."

By the time they got to town, the grandfather and the grandson were both carrying the donkey.

The point is that no matter what you do, you will never please everybody. Just accelerate with your life, get yourself back up again and do something. When great victories are won through ordinary people, there's no question as to whom should receive the glory.

God chose the foolish things… so that NO FLESH should glory in His presence (**1 CORINTHIANS 1:29**).

If most of us would have been born above average, we may have not been giving God the glory. We possibly may have BEEN glorifying ourselves in God's presence.

Our assignment needs to welcome HIS alignment. Be open to what God wants from you in order to get up and get moving again.

You don't have to be "COLORFUL" to be "CREDIBLE." If your credit score has gone down with God, it's okay. File bankruptcy (repentance) with Him and let Him restore your credit back in the 800-900's. God is not looking for brains, he's looking for heart. Yes, you may have failed, you may have made big mistakes that men can't forgive. But, it's not the forgiveness of men that you need, you just need the forgiveness of Jesus Christ. And He is always just a knock away! Jesus said in Matthew 7:7: *Knock, and the door you are knocking on will be opened to you.*

> *Our assignment needs to welcome HIS alignment.*
> *—FF*

A pastor was dying. He sent a message for his doctor and his lawyer, both church members, to come to his home. When they arrived at his house, they were ushered up to his bedroom.

As they entered the room, the pastor held out his hands and motioned for them to sit on each side of the bed.

The pastor held both their hands, took a deep breath, he smiled and stared at the ceiling.

For a time, no one said anything. Both the doctor and lawyer were touched and flattered that their pastor would ask them to be with him during his final moment.

They were also puzzled, because their pastor had never given them any indication that he even knew them.

They both remembered his many long, uncomfortable sermons about greed, covetousness, and their sinful behavior that made them squirm in their seats.

Finally the doctor church member said, "Pastor, why did you ask the two of us to come?"

Their pastor mustered up some strength, took another deep breath, then said very weakly, "Jesus died between two thieves right before he died and that's how I want to go too."

As you are about to close this book and hand it to someone else who needs it, there will always be people who, in their own minds, consider you **dis.con.tinued.** One of the thieves on the cross thought that about Christ to his very last breath on the cross. Don't let those kinds of people invite you to their pity party while they die.

The problem a person could have with using face time and Facebook together is that they can become "two faced."

Go ahead, just be like Jesus. While people will NEVER stop

> *The problem a person could have with using face time and Facebook together is that they can become "two faced." —FF*

talking about you, choose to die with a smile on your face because of what Christ says about you, not what the world says about you.

As long as we are living with humans we are always at the chance of being **dis.con.tinued.** We are not dealing with **product** or **paper,** but with **people.** Product and paper are made up of materials, people of all race and color are made up of feelings. Real people with real feelings are always free to *feel* what they want to feel and judge who they want to judge. Many times we are the ones being judged.

God gave us all our individual capacity of feelings. And because people have that right, we are always in the danger of being labeled as **dis.con.tinued.**

My father and I eventually reunited and had a relationship that was extremely precious! I was not just his son but his pastor. I was honored to have led him in the sinner's prayer and he began attending church with me. He was able to see his son preach with his own eyes. He had heard of me being a preacher and was always proud of it. However, towards the end of his vicious fight with lung cancer he was able to see with his own eyes that he had produced a pastor as a son. When my father passed, he did so with the peace of God surrounding him full circle, knowing without a doubt that he was on his way to heaven.

Remember this, if we would just remove the word **dis** from **continued,** and add the words to-be, then we would go from **dis.con.tinued** – **to.be.continued**.

Look for my next book titled

to

be

continued.

Respectfully,
Fernando E. Franco Sr.

NOTES

Introduction:

Dis.con.tinued: Definition used from the
New Oxford American Dictionary

Chapter one:

Hater-isim: https://www.urbandictionary.com/
James 3:1: NIV Translation

Chapter two:

Hebrews 4:15: NIV Translation
James 3:1: NIV Translation
Psalm 55:12-15: NLT Translation
Statistics about pastors burnout:
https://praisedc.com/1676312/
why-are-so-many-pastors-committing-suicide/
John 10:10: TLT Translation
Haterisim, the truth and symptoms: Urban dictionary
Luke 22:39-45: TLB Translation
John 6:60-62: TLB Translation

John 7:40-43: TLB Translation

Luke 2:39-52: TLB Translation

Luke 23: 39-41: NLT Translation

Matthew 16:13-17: NIV Translation

John 20:25: NIV Translation

Chapter three:

James 3:8-10:The Message Translation

Glossolitis: Why churches die? by Mac
Brunson & Ergun Caner

Mark 5:1-5: NIV Translation (Emphasis added: Jesus)

1 Corinthians 14:5: NIV Translation

1 Corinthians 14:2: NIV Translation

1 Corinthians 14:18: NIV Translation

1 Corinthians 14:14: NIV Translation

Numbers 12:1-2: NIV Translation

Numbers 12:2: NIV Translation

Proverbs 6:16,17: NIV Translation

1 Thessalonians 5:17: NIV Translation

Tongues of fire: Speaking in tongues and its
significance for the church by: Larry Christenson

Four patterns to diagnose if you have *tongues of liars*:
Why churches die?by Mac Brunson & Ergun Caner

Proverbs 11:13 : NLT Translation

Proverbs 18:8 : MSG Translation

Proverbs 26:20 : NIV Translation

Proverbs 26:24-26: MSG Translation

Chapter four:

Amos 3:12: ISV Translation

Luke 22:39-45: NLT

Job 8:7: GW Translation

Isaiah 53:11: NLT

Ringley bros & Barnum & Bailey: https://en.wikipedia.org/wiki/Ringling_Bros._and_Barnum_%26_Bailey_Circus

Chapter five:

Facts of Jesse Jackson: https://en.wikipedia.org/wiki/Jesse_Jackson

Facts of Nick Vujicic: https://en.wikipedia.org/wiki/Nick_Vujicic

Israel Houghton and Chad Veach: https://www.youtube.com/watch?v=mGXMH2u7k3A

Tiger Woods wins Masters 2019: (https://www.msn.com/en-us/news/other/masters-2019-tiger-woods-finally-provides-major-moment-weve-been-waiting-for/ar-BBVVNje)

Chapter six:

Happy people are so focused on their own goals, they don't have time to look around to see how everybody else is living. Happy people don't get intimidated by others, they get *inspired*: You can You will by: Joel Osteen

Chapter eight:

A star is born: **https://www.imdb.com/ title/tt1517451/plotsummary**

John Walsh: https://en.wikipedia.org/ wiki/John_Walsh_(television_host)

Chapter nine:

Corinthians 1:26, 27 (The message translation)

Visit our online Church Growth Material website at

https://www.onlinechurchgrowthmaterial.com/

CPSIA information can be obtained
at www.ICGtesting.com
Printed in the USA
FSHW020117170521
81482FS